Israel Jacobson

THE FOUNDER OF THE REFORM MOVEMENT IN JUDAISM

ISRAEL JACOBSSOHN

Geheim- Finanzrath und Präsident des
Königl. Westphäl. Consistoriums mosaischer
Religion.

From Sulamith, II. No. I

Israel Jacobson

THE FOUNDER OF THE REFORM MOVEMENT IN JUDAISM

by

Jacob R. Marcus

Hebrew Union College Press

Cincinnati   1972

SBN 0-87820-000-2

Library of Congress Card Number: 74-187950

Manufactured in the United States of America

To
Rose Brody
and
Joseph M. Brody

Preface

It was in 1928, on the centennial of the death of Israel Jacobson, that I wrote this biography of the founder of the Reform Movement in Judaism. It appeared originally in Volume XXXVIII of the *Yearbook of the Central Conference of American Rabbis* and immediately thereafter was republished as an offprint.

Germany was still the center of the Science of Judaism in the 1920's, but Reform Judaism had yet to make its mark in the larger context of World Jewry. A great deal of water has since passed over the dam. Central and East European Jewry has been practically annihilated, while Liberal Judaism has become an international religious movement with a vigorous synagogal life in nearly every corner of the globe. I think it no exaggeration to maintain that what Jacobson began in early nineteenth-century Germany is today the largest liberal religious fellowship in the world.

The year 1968 was the two-hundredth anniversary of Israel Jacobson's birth, and it is only fitting that this biography, so long out of print, be again made available. I believe, however, that there are other, more compelling reasons to reprint the book at this time. Jacobson initiated his activities as a religious reformer in the generation of the French Revolution and its testamentary legatee, the Emperor Napoleon. In those years, a whole new world was dawning for the Jews of Central Europe. For the first time in well over a millennium, they faced the problem of adjusting themselves to the bouleversement of political, social, and economic emancipation, but spiritual, religious emancipation, too, was inevitable— and irresistible.

Today, in the last third of the twentieth century, Reform Jews on every continent find themselves confronting still another "Revolution," a ferment which threatens to explode every value the Reformers of earlier generations held dear. The theology, the liturgy, the traditional Jewish morality, even the very raison d'être of Judaism—all these must answer to sharp challenge. Indeed, almost every human and humanistic value finds itself challenged in this age of nuclear energy when the new-old empires of the twentieth century are fighting for their lives and when new political forces rising in the East promise to shatter much that the Western World has held sacred. It is quite likely that radical changes—whether of a liberal or a reactionary character— will, in the years ahead, profoundly affect Reform Judaism and its adherents. Given all this, the life and struggle of the first Reform Jew, the first Jewish religious "radical," may be of more than passing interest to his spiritual heirs.

Some of the articles and essays which I was not privileged to consult in the 1920's have now become available to me and are incorporated into this revised and corrected edition. The work still remains the most exhaustive study of Jacobson and is, I fondly believe, authentic, detailed, and adequately documented. If Jacobson were to return tomorrow, he might well raise an eyebrow at my evaluation of his personality and his career, but he would certainly be gratified at the success of the Reformation which he sparked.

Some acknowledgments are in order at this point. I deeply appreciate the permission given me by the Central Conference of American Rabbis to reprint the book, and I am more grateful than I can say to the Alumni Association of the Hebrew Union College-Jewish Institute of Religion for its generosity in making a new edition possible. My good friend, Dr. Stanley F. Chyet, Associate Director of the American Jewish Archives, has been pressing me for years to undertake republication of Jacobson's biography, and I am much indebted to him for speeding its rebirth. Like Dr. Chyet, Dr. Abraham I. Shinedling, my dear friend and colleague of many decades, has carefully read the text, offered many valuable suggestions, and, with his usual thoroughness, prepared a detailed index. I am only too happy to acknowledge his many kindnesses to me.

JACOB R. MARCUS

Hebrew Union College
Cincinnati, Ohio
January, 1971

CONTENTS

1. Jacobson's Background

Israel Jacobson was so much an object of contention in the past that he could not be evaluated without prejudice. He had to be dead for a century before an objective study of his life and aims could be undertaken. First of all, he arranged a Reform Jewish service. He prepared the way for a Reform Jewish theology. This made him the founder of Reform, and an object of sharp criticism on the part of the historians, most of whom were opposed to the interpretation of Judaism which grew out of his teachings. Conservative and Orthodox Jewish historians, therefore, did not care to write of him in detail. The Reformers neglected him because greater figures appeared on the horizon to occupy their attention. Thus there was no adequate biography of the man. The descriptions of him that appeared were touched by partisanship or limited themselves to but one phase of his varied career. This essay will attempt to interpret the man in all his activities in the light of the age in which he flourished and will seek to evaluate his historic importance for his own and for a later time. The study is justified, I believe, not only because there has been no other attempt to give a full-length portrait of him, but also because all preceding writers have looked upon Jacobson merely as a reformer of externals in Jewish religious life. They failed to point out that his changes were based on a philosophy which was bound ultimately to have a radical effect on some of the fundamental principles of traditional Judaism.[1]

Jacobson, probably more than the average man, was influenced by the thinking of his time. He came out of a fine, strong, Orthodox Jewish environment and found himself in the midst of one of the most fascinating epochs of European history and culture: the period of Frederick the Great, the French Revolution, Napoleon, and the Germany of the Restoration of 1815. The life of his less fortunate fellow-Jews certainly seemed narrow, unfree, unprogressive to him. The Gentile world about him offered a rich culture, art, and philosophy. He was so deeply impressed by the thinking of his time that he overestimated its cultural value and underestimated the capacities of Judaism. His attitude as a Jew was always an apologetic one. He honestly believed that the Gentile world about him was superior to his Jewish one and that Jewry, without sacrifice of principle, of course, would have to surrender itself to the beautiful new age.

Every thought of Jacobson was permeated by the philosophy of the Enlightenment in all its manifold expressions. It dominated him completely despite the fact that this orientation had been under constant fire for decades. Jacobson was oblivious to any criticism of it because he would not, he could not, recognize any other discipline. It was the only philosophy of life which permitted him to be both modern and Jewish. He could not give it up or deny it.

The Enlightenment was a common-sense philosophy that conceived of the universe and all history as something which could be made quite clear to reason because everything grew out of reason. The adoption of this point of view had to dispel all mystery, do away with all superstition, and illuminate everything by the torch of reason. Knowledge had to become the possession of all people. The mind had to be made free, it had to rule every act. Reason was the only road to salvation. Reason, which ruled the world of Nature, was accorded an almost religious veneration. Yet, despite the preponderance of rationality in the German Enlightenment, its background was always moral and religious.

The Enlightenment was determined to free itself from all traditional slavery, to take the future into its own hands. It proclaimed an exultant belief in an inevitable advance to freedom, dignity, and human happiness. It taught a respect for human rights and made popular the words humanity, good will, natural rights, liberty, equality, and brotherhood. It was the philosophy of unlimited optimism. This world was the best of all possible worlds. It was an age "when God was a father, and nature a mother, and all was for the best in a scientific universe."[2]

It was filled with a sober realization of the individual's responsibility to determine his own life. It courageously sought to apply to the whole field of history the gauge of critical reason in order to reform the state, society, economic life, religion, and education.

This philosophy reflected itself on the eighteenth-century political scene in the form of an Enlightened Despotism. The logical, mechanized, bureaucratic state was intellectually related to the rationalism and moralism of the Enlightenment. The ideal type of an enlightened despot was Frederick the Great, and it was in his age and in his land that Jacobson spent the formative decade of his life. He lived for almost twenty years under the scepter of the astute Frederick. Jacobson grew up in a police state where everything was done at the command of one individual, but ostensibly for the good of all. Frederick's subjects were to be legislated into intelligent and good citizenship. Every act of the individual was carefully prescribed and regulated with clocklike precision. The philosopher of the German Enlightenment, Wolff of Halle, declared that the state had the right and the duty to protect the mass of unenlightened people from error and to interfere even in their most intimate private affairs in order to educate them properly. Jacobson himself was politically in sympathy with French constitutional liberalism, but the form of governmental administration that attracted him was certainly the absolutistic one. It was efficient and appealed to the businessman in him.

Jacobson lived through stirring times, times that made men think carefully. He saw the partition of Poland, the Tolerance Edict of Joseph II of Austria which granted Jewry extended privileges, the publication of the United States Constitution, the French Revolution, and the emancipation of French Jewry. He saw the onrush of the French revolutionary armies with their radical slogans, the rise of the great Napoleon and his promises of universal liberty.

His point of view in Jewish matters was not provincial, for in his youth Halberstadt, his native town, sheltered probably the largest Jewish community in Prussia and teemed with a vigorous religious and economic life.[3]

The religious counterpart of the Enlightenment was deism. Deism in its broadest sense was rational religion. It was the first attempt to render religion acceptable to progressive and scientific thinkers. It preached rational metaphysics, God, immortality, and freedom of will. Its whole ethical system was logical, reasonable. Deism stressed the ideal of tolerance and respect for that which was human and humane.

The moralistic principles shared by most deistic writers influenced Jacobson very much. According to these writers, the way to honor God and at the same time achieve the happiness that God desired man to attain was to lead a virtuous life. In the world to come, God would work out the inequalities of this life so that virtue might ultimately be rewarded. Jacobson probably believed, with Voltaire, that there was an intuitive universal religion common to all mankind and that the customs and rites of the various religious systems were encrustations on the true religion. True religion was, therefore, a return to the original, uncorrupted faith.[4]

Deism, which in Protestant Germany had become the religion of the cultured middle class, laid no emphasis on asceticism, the cult, or ceremonial. Since only the natural and reasonable could be right, intellectual domination through otherworldly views was at an end. Religion was made this-worldly. The aims of life were concentrated on this rational world. Only that which was really useful, helpful, moral was worth keeping. Church standards were thrown overboard. A sharp distinction was made between education and the Church. Law and morals were clearly distinguished from theology.

A powerful influence in the religious development of the German Enlightenment was the Berlin school of Popular Philosophers. These intellectuals wrote a great deal about the moral improvement of man and immortality. Their "moral periodicals" demanded a complete change in the inner man. The social and private life of the individual was to be improved; education had to be reformed; women could not be kept in ignorance. The Berlin thinkers placed vital human interests above theological quarrels. They gave morality a basis independent of dogmatic creed, and they insisted that toleration be granted to men of all faiths. Their enthusiasm for morality was a healthy reaction to the skepticism of the French materialists.

Among the Enlightenment leaders was the Jew Mendelssohn, probably the strongest individual influence on the intellectual development of Israel Jacobson. The young autodidact had a profound respect for this sage, who was so distinguished for his fine moral sympathies and his enthusiasm for religious and political freedom. Jewry was proud of Mendelssohn. He was the incarnation of the victory of the Enlightenment over narrowness and prejudice. Enlightenment and deism came into Jewish life most directly through this man. In practice, Mendelssohn, the Enlightener, had remained an Orthodox Jew. Intellectually, however, he and many a Jew after him were attracted to deism because it, too, was antitrinitarian and posited original virtue and the moral freedom of man. Jacobson was directly influenced by Mendelssohn's contrast between moralism and legalism, religion and the ceremonial law. The Protestant theologians in sympathy with the popular philosophy which Mendelssohn fostered were Spalding, Teller, and Semler, all of whom influenced the Jewish life of the time.[5]

Semler went so far as to renounce the traditional doctrine of inspiration and to speak of the gradual development of the canon and the unequal value of its different parts. That only was of divine origin which served for moral improvement. The rest was only for local and temporal accommodation and served without contemporary significance. Touches of this thought are found in the Confession of Faith of Jacobson. These Protestant clergymen, fired by a reforming zeal, changed their preaching, hymns, and liturgy to conform to the new ideas. Their sermons taught the passing of dogmatic values and the rise of a new emphasis on morals and a beneficent Providence.

Deism was not the only religious influence on German life at this time. The old, immutable, dogmatic Protestant orthodoxy was still powerful, and the strong pietistic movement of the early eighteenth century still lived in the hearts of many. Pietism taught religious individualism, piety in works, an inner, heartfelt, religious sympathy, asceticism, and mysticism. Jacobson had no sympathy for this school of thought and was apparently uninfluenced by it, although it flourished in neighboring Westphalia. Yet his background in his father's home was certainly one of Jewish pietism, and because it was the soil in which he was first nurtured, he was never able to escape its influence. He was enmeshed in Jewish pietism.

In the last quarter of the eighteenth century, as Jacobson was growing and developing, new movements arose in literature and in philosophy to oppose the shallowness of eighteenth-century rationalism. Jacobson was not untouched by them. Whatever agreed with his basic enlightenment views he assimilated within himself; whatever did not appeal to him he threw overboard. In 1779, Gotthold Ephraim Lessing's *Nathan the Wise* appeared. The enlightened Jew Lessing had created was the embodiment of the spirit of a free mankind and an undogmatic religion of human love. The thoughts of this man, who was fighting for the spiritual and intellectual freedom of mankind, appealed to Jacobson. He was certainly not uninfluenced by Lessing's independent attitude toward traditional theology.

Rousseau, Lessing, and Herder were all known to him. Their appeal for deeper and more intense religious feeling, their unconscious reproach of the superficiality and inadequacy of rationalism do not seem to have touched him. Rousseau's denial that the development of reason brought with it the perfection of man was not accepted by him. But his political principles of democracy and equality for all men were incorporated into Jacobson's political ideas. Herder's and Lessing's feeling for the importance of a sense of historicity left him cold. The humanitarianism of all three appealed to him mightily. There is a passage of Herder often quoted in the generation of Jacobson, and I am sure that it was known to him. It expresses, better than any passage I know, the ideals of Jacobson. It was the pabulum on which he fed. "What a prospect it would be," says Herder,

> to see the Jews, an intelligent people, devoted to the culture of the sciences, the welfare of the state which protects them, to other purposes of value to mankind, and to have them in their deeds and thinking, too, completely humanized! Gone the old proud national prejudices, thrown away the customs which for our time and constitution, even for our climate, are antiquated. Let them not work as slaves on a Colosseum, but as associates of cultured peoples on the greatest and most beautiful Colosseum: the building of the sciences, the complete culture of mankind. Not on the naked hills of Palestine, that narrow, desolate land, but everywhere let their spiritual Temple rise from amidst the ruins. Let all nations honor with them and they with all nations the Creator of the world in that they develop and exalt his picture: reason, wisdom, generosity, and kindness to humanity. They cannot be brought to honor and morality through the granting of new business opportunities; they can raise themselves to this height only through pure, humanitarian, scientific and civil accomplishments. Their Palestine is there where they live and are an influence for good: everywhere.[6]

"A time will come," says Herder in one of his famous books,

> when people in Europe will no longer ask who is a Jew or a Christian, for the Jew also will live according to European standards and will contribute to the welfare of the state from which he has been shut out only by a barbaric constitution.[7]

The Storm and Stress movement now broke loose. It was a revolt against reason, against discipline in life and art. It asked for a return to pure nature and originality as the individual conceived it. It was irrationalism and subjectivism run riot. It was tired of the unimaginative sobriety and the empty self-complacency of rationalism: imagination and feeling, not only reason, had a right to life. But this passionate idealization of the undisciplined in life had no appeal for a man who believed in law and order, who was a successful businessman with a family in his early twenties.

The classical period of German literature appealed to him as little. It came too late for him. I do not find that he absorbed any new ideas after his twentieth year. I do not think that he understood this new movement, although both the Enlightenment and Classicism preached the same goal: humanity. Jacobson believed in this ideal as did all his contemporaries. The pages of their journal, *Sulamith,* are studded with this beautiful word. But he came to it through the Enlightenment which taught the brotherhood of man because of a common humanity. The concept of humanity of this Neo-Classicism was different. Its ideal was aristocratic and historic. It meant a renascence of an idealized Greek culture and education. It meant a perfect harmony and development of the individual's emotions and intellectual capacities. It meant a recognition of the dignity inherent in man as man. This ideal was to be attained, not through religion and morals, but through aesthetics. This was impossible for a man who was so strongly fortified with morals both from the Jewish and the philosophic side. Although Jacobson's philosophic sources had a system of aesthetics, he had no real understanding of this concept. He may have used the term, but he meant decorum and the amenities.

This Neo-Classicism had much that he believed in. It also taught education, freedom, tolerance, and truth, but this he had already from the whole preceding Enlightenment philosophy and did not have to turn to the young Goethe and Schiller for it. This new teaching was after all a world that would have to remain closed to him, for it took for granted a certain amount of classical training. He possessed none. It unconsciously emphasized the line between educated and uneducated, and this could not appeal to a man who was an autodidact and, in spite of wealth, unspoiled and unsnobbish. It could not appeal to a man to whom the ideal of equality, fraternity, and liberty was something very real.

The Storm and Stress movement of the sixties and seventies found its continuity, in a way, in the new German Romanticism. There appears to be no trace in Jacobson of this great movement in thought, literature, and religion. This ideal, first aesthetic and literary, soon became religious. The emphasis on feeling and imagination soon led to a new mysticism. The influence of Spinoza made itself felt here, too, and soon Romanticism was distinguished by an aesthetic, mystical, pantheistic piety. It wanted to abolish the laws of the rational thinking mind and to enter into the beautiful confusion of imagination and into the original chaos of human nature. It asked for the understanding of everything through the emotions. It was the very opposite of the clear and antimystical and objective Enlightenment. Jacobson would have none of it. Berlin was dominated by it before Jacobson even became a figure of note, but he had no sympathy or understanding for a teaching that exulted in man rather than in humanity. Kant, in his criticism of the rational theology of the Enlightenment and the claims of reason, was, like Fichte, only a name to Jacobson.[8]

Jacobson was bound hand and foot to the Enlightenment philosophy because he was a Jew and because of his education. His meagre, simple education, his practical, common-sense training, flourished in rationalism. It was a middle-class philosophy for a middle-class man. It was the only philosophy that had a place for him as a Jew. It was the philosophy of natural rights which brought emancipation for the Jew in the French Revolution and would yet, he hoped, bring freedom to the Jew everywhere. This is the only movement that insisted on a respect for human rights, for "liberty of conscience and worship, for equal opportunity and economic freedom, for representative government and equality of all individuals before the law."

Jacobson, enthralled by the broad humanitarian, cosmopolitan views of eighteenth-century liberalism, went forward into the nineteenth century to help his people. He brought with him an eighteenth-century philosophy of life that he wished to serve for the nineteenth. He did not realize the inadequacy of his teachings. The whole Enlightenment movement lacked clearly defined principles and was without religious depth. There was no capacity in it to grasp the significance of the Great and the Deep and the Beautiful in life. There was an overloading of intellectualism, a fatigue of religious feeling that left unsatisfied the deepest needs of the religious nature. Mysteries and ceremonies were thrown overboard and much religious feeling with them. The institutions and the mechanics of religion were undermined by the Enlightenment because it was antiauthoritarian and antisupernaturalist. The struggles of the deeply religious soul for a spiritual adjustment to the universe were ignored. There was no primeval strength in this reasonable religion. It was the artificial product of thinkers. Before Jacobson ever attempted any reforms of Jewish religious life, he came to his tasks with a rationalistic prejudice against the authority and the ceremonial of normative Jewish tradition. This whole movement was narrow, without perspective, because it lacked a sense of historicity. Jacobson and his friends set up demands and concepts without any consideration of realities. They believed in concepts merely because they had been evolved logically out of the mind. They had no appreciation of the enormous attraction of historic tradition. They had no understanding of the distinct historic character of individuals and peoples. They did not realize the gap between secular humanitarianism on one side and Jewish religious particularism on the other. They attempted to sweep away deeply rooted illogical prejudice with perfect syllogisms. It was all noble, but quixotic—and ineffectual.

2. Youth

Jacobson can best be understood by understanding his family. The influence of his father can be traced throughout his career. The Seesen temple, one of the crowning achievements of his life, was built and dedicated to the memory of his father.[1] For a rather intimate picture of the father's life we are indebted to the fascinating work of the Protestant minister Karl Witte, who preached at Lochau, near Halle. Witte addressed his book to all "noble and good people."[2]

Witte, like many Protestant and Catholic clergymen, was profoundly touched by the humanitarian spirit of the age. He believed that God was not only the God of the Christians, but also of the Jews and of all mankind. He wrote the history of Israel Jacob, the father, not only as a memorial to a good man, but also to remove from the hearts of the peasants unchristian prejudices against the Jews. He hoped, too, through the sale of his book, to raise money for the organ that he needed for his church. Jacobson had already given him some and had also furnished him with information regarding his father.

"The rich Jacob" who had lived in Halberstadt in the first half of the eighteenth century was the founder of the family fortunes and traditions. Unfortunately, he had lost his wealth, and the burden of support soon fell on the shoulders of his only son Israel, the father of Israel Jacobson. Israel's struggle to make good in the world of business is a fascinating one. He had received some education, more than the average young man of his day, and this knowledge stood him in good stead. His ability to read and write and reckon and his sterling qualities of character brought him to the attention of the Abbot of Huysburg, who had tried him by offering him swine's flesh. Israel's rise to power and wealth after his romantic sufferings was rapid. He was appointed purveyor to the monastery and became known as "the honest cloister-Jew." He acquired his later wealth through trade and banking. His reputation for honesty was proverbial. His charities knew no bounds of creed or race. He kept a very careful account of his various charities and never gave less than one-tenth of his income every year to the needy.[3] He lived very modestly and dressed quietly. There was no ostentation in his living. He was very pious and scrupulously observed all the laws and customs. His formula for success in life was characteristic: be diligent, be thrifty, trust in God and pray to Him. Honor and love your parents and those over you, and help the poor. These are all old-fashioned ideals. He was not sympathetic to beggars, but always ready to help the poor. He contributed to all the charities in Halberstadt and particularly approved of supporting institutions. He was eager to further the study of the Torah and was willing to help transient Jewish scholars. He had promised to give ten thousand talers to the poor after his death, but died in 1803 at the age of seventy-five without doing so. His son Israel Jacobson, knowing of his father's intention, immediately carried it out by giving the money and calling the foundation "Israel's Wreath of Honor."

Israel Jacob, the father, was distinguished not only through his charities, but also through his activity for the Jewish community. He soon became one of its officers and devoted himself to the task of reducing the community debt. At times he even advanced his own money. These sums were not always returned to him. He helped Jews to secure patents so that they might marry, and it is not improbable that he had influence with the Prussian and other German state authorities. The parental zeal for all types of charitable activity, for the Jewish religion, for Jewish communal life, for the welfare of Jewry as a whole goes far to explain the interests and the career of the son.[4]

Israel Jacobson, the only son of Israel Jacob, was born in Halberstadt, October 17, 1768.[5] His father was then already in his fortieth year and had attained riches and position. Jacobson was thus born into a family of wealth and tradition. His early training was strongly Orthodox, and he was given a fairly good Hebrew education. He was taught Bible, Mishnah, and Talmud. It is hard to determine his proficiency in these branches, but he certainly had some understanding of rabbinic literature. He wrote and read Hebrew letters. The professors at the neighboring University of Helmstedt looked upon him as a Hebrew scholar, but of course they were poor judges. The father did not give him a particularly good secular education. He was taught some German and French. Even in later life, his knowledge of German was not perfect.[6] His father probably still spoke Yiddish at home. In no sense was Jacobson an educated man. He realized this himself and never stopped studying as he grew up. He was self-taught. His education was unsystematic. The father, who may have been a good Hebraist, wished to make a rabbi of his only son. But this interest did not hold the young Jacobson very long. He became absorbed in German literature and the world about him. He read Lessing and Mendelssohn. He studied or heard about the ideals of Rousseau and other French philosophers. His view of the world became broader.

The rabbinic ideal probably seemed narrow to him. It certainly offered little scope to a man who was very ambitious. He gave it up and threw himself wholeheartedly into the world of business.[7]

3.   Brunswick

Halberstadt prepared Jacobson for the world, but it was at Brunswick, the capital of the duchy of the same name, that he tested himself. He was now only eighteen years of age, but so able that he attracted the attention of the Kammeragent Herz Samson. Samson was a respected financier who had done much to build up the credit of the Duchy of Brunswick and as a result enjoyed the friendship of Duke Charles William Ferdinand. The eighteen-year-old Halberstadter married Mink, the daughter of Samson. This union of two wealthy families was a most happy one.[1]

Young Jacobson's rise to great wealth and power was rapid. His family connections gave him advantages; his abilities enabled him to make the most of them. He won and retained the benevolent favor of the duke. This was not an easy task. Charles William Ferdinand was not the most pleasant of rulers, yet the relations between the two were most amicable. Jacobson must have had a wholesome respect for this man who was over thirty years his senior and had enjoyed a distinguished career under the great Frederick. It was to be expected that the influence of the duke on the impressionable young Halberstadter would be strong. Charles had been a favorite nephew of Frederick the Great and, like his illustrious master, he, too, was a believer in an enlightened despotism as a method of administration, a policy that gave little opportunity for individual expression. In his younger years, he had received a good education and in his travels had visited

17

the great Voltaire. Even later he was not out of sympathy
with progressive ideas. He was no reactionary or spendthrift
princeling. Education keenly interested him, and so he established good schools in the land. The new trend in pedagogy
that was tried out in the neighboring Dessau by Basedow
appealed to him. Charles was interested in church reform,
too. He wanted changes in the liturgy and catechism, but
could accomplish little in the face of the opposition that his
ideas met.

Jacobson's financial operations carried him into the different German states and neighboring lands. He met rulers
and people of distinction; he learned to believe in himself. He
understood and enjoyed the amenities of polite society; he was
at home in courts. His integrity was evident, and when his
father-in-law died it was quite natural that this fine, impres-
sive-looking Jew of twenty-six should succeed him at court.
He became Kammeragent and Landrabbiner of the Weser
district.[2]

Jacobson was interested in his people. In his travels he had
learned to know the dismal state of his fellow-Jews. He had
noticed everywhere the bad educational conditions and the
undignified religious services. He felt he was called upon to
make a great reform in Jewish life. He believed that his
people were behind the times because of the persecution of
the states in which they found themselves. In order to make
them like their fellowmen in their cultural life, in their
religious observances, in their synagogal services, in their
communal life, yes, even in their inner moral life, it was
imperative that there be a reform, that is, a change in the
sense of a closer approach to modern habits. It was imperative, he felt, that Jewish education be improved through the
establishment of the proper type of school—one built along

rationalistic lines. If there was a moral decay in Jewry—and he believed there was—it could be stopped through the proper instruction of the young.[3]

His interest in education was primary. Here Jacobson was dependent on a double influence, Jewish and non-Jewish. General educational ideas had changed tremendously in Germany in the century in which he was born. He lived within a stone's throw of the great sources and scenes of this cultural revolution. Theology and the Latin tongue had been dethroned, modern philosophy, science, and a secular attitude were supreme. Freedom of thought was gaining ground.

Ten years after Jacobson was born, in his native town of Halberstadt, von Rochow helped establish the first training college for teachers. In Halle and Goettingen, just a few miles away, the new ideas in education found their fullest expression. In Helmstedt, which later gave Jacobson a degree, Wiedeburg, his friend, had established a teachers' training school. A new, educated middle class was arising in Germany. An earnest attempt was made to do away with the deplorable educational conditions in existence, and by the end of the eighteenth century Germany had made great strides.

Though Jacobson was unaffected by the naturalism of Rousseau and Herder in religion, he was very much influenced by their naturalism in education. Rousseau's educational ideals influenced him strongly as he grew up, albeit indirectly, through the teachings of Basedow, the educationist, who effected a synthesis of the teachings of Rousseau and Wolff, the philosopher of the German Enlightenment. Rousseau wanted to further the full and unfettered individuality of the child by the development of all its powers. He wanted to turn aside from a narrow pedantry. He insisted on the real and practical in life, on clearness, on individual instruction. Basedow carried out the ideas of Rousseau. In Dessau, in 1774, he founded the Philanthropinum to give young folks an education that was in touch with real life, an education that was in accordance with human nature and the spirit of the age. In short, he pleaded for an understanding of humanity. He, too, united the principle of a "natural" education with utility. The individual was thus to be prepared to be a full member of society. It is interesting that this type of individualism in education should have appealed to Jacobson, who was by nature a believer in regimentation. The apparent contradiction may be resolved when we realize that the ultimate function of this type of individualistic training was to make all young men and women useful members of the broader society.

Jacobson was certainly influenced by the new educational ideas which were so well-known in his own immediate neighborhood. He himself was known for his interest in the University of Helmstedt and for his association with academicians. He had that respect for the learned that always characterizes the self-taught.

The decisive factor, however, in the career of Jacobson is that he was a Mendelssohnian. The efforts of Mendelssohn to bring enlightenment, his desire to assimilate contemporary secular culture, impressed itself only upon a few leaders. But these devoted disciples, men like Jacobson, carried on his work. The best instrument for this purpose, they decided, was the school. Through this institution they hoped to influence the younger generation. It is not accidental, therefore, that there arose a series of Jewish schools from the latter days of Mendelssohn on into the nineteenth century.[4] Zunz called the quarter of a century between 1783 and 1807 the age of

education.[5] It was during this period that efforts were made
to improve the education of the young and to make them
look and act like their non-Jewish contemporaries. Mendelssohn had once cried out bitterly that his people were so
distant from culture that one could almost despair of any
improvement.[6] Jewish education in Jacobson's day was still
in a deplorable condition. Particularly in the small towns,
there were no opportunities for education. Some parents were
not even interested. Instruction, when given, was limited to
some knowledge of Hebrew reading by incompetent individuals broken on the wheel of fortune.

Jacobson looked to education as the key to all Jewish hopes.
The school would raise the Jew mentally, morally, socially,
religiously. Through the religious teachings imparted to the
children, he believed he would be able to influence even the
older generation. Despite his rationalist prejudices, he had
no conscious desire to leave Orthodoxy; he wished to em-
phasize· the Hebrew language. Education would teach the
Jew to be rational and thus bring about a change for the
better in his religious life. Knowledge would bring him closer
to humanity and show him the inadequacy of his own way
of living and doing business. Education would fit him into his
surroundings and prepare him for the emancipation which
was sure to come some day. Once the Jew was free, he
would be in a position to desert the petty trading which had
degraded him and to enter into agricultural and industrial
pursuits. Jacobson was particularly desirous of educating poor
Jewish lads. He wanted them to engage in something useful.
He wanted to teach them an honest trade that they might
have a fair chance in life and not go wrong and disgrace their
people. It is noteworthy that he was not interested in having
the Jews go to the general elementary schools. He probably

thought it inexpedient because of the difficulties involved in religious instruction. The desire to retain confessional schools always characterized Jacobson. He did, however, wish the Jewish schools to maintain a standard as high as the others.[7]

Yet the Jewish interpretation of life was not emphasized in his educational program. The average child was Jewish enough—too Jewish. The problem was to modernize him. The state was to be shown that the Jew could be modernized, and this realization should induce it to emancipate the Jew civilly. An educated Jew would convince the world that Jews are worthy people, and Gentiledom would be so impressed that it would remove the laws that had made it impossible for them to live naturally and properly. This desire to make the Jew presentable as a "cultured person" was very strong in the first decade of the nineteenth century—a period when the Jew was looked askance at, not only by the ignorant masses, but also by great leaders like Goethe.[8]

Secular education, therefore, was for Jacobson a means to effect a complete inner reformation of the individual Jew and to make him acceptable to the world at large. It never seems to have occurred to him in these early days that the state might not care to assimilate even educated and cultured Jews. The realization of this sad truth in the last years of his stay in Brunswick almost broke his heart.

Jacobson was moved by the broadest humanitarian views. He was prepared to accept Christian children in the Jewish schools to show the world how well Jew and Christian could get along together. He was going to teach the Christian tolerance. He wanted to start with impressionable children to eliminate prejudice. Since Jews and Christians must ultimately associate with each other, he thought it advisable to begin this association in school. These are the ideas which moved

Jacobson. He could best serve his people by educating them.[9]

Jacobson was determined to lead the way by establishing a school and selected Seesen, a small town, as the spot of its location. Seesen was chosen, possibly, because of the sympathy of the official, Zincken, who lived there, or because he may have wished to isolate himself from larger Jewish communities like Halberstadt and Brunswick in order that the school might not be exposed to any influence, except his and his friends'.[10] The cost of establishing and endowing it involved what was for those days a very large sum of money. He found it was easier to talk of establishing a school than actually to build one. The Gentiles of the town protested; the magistrates were indignant that the school was not to be controlled by them but by Zincken, who, in turn, was responsible directly to the duke. In consonance with the newer ideas the founder had decided to erect an industrial and agricultural school. But the townsmen were appalled at the thought that he might purchase a farm in conjunction with his school and raise the price of land from which they as tenants made their living. That was the end of the agricultural school.

Jacobson wanted the confidence of the citizens. He was shrewd enough to realize that without their moral support he would always be handicapped. Then, again, he wanted to be liked. Opposition irritated him; lack of popularity cut him to the quick. Through his generous gifts to the city and its poor, through the force of his probity, he gradually won over the people of the town. Sentiment now swung so far in his direction that his very opponents there encouraged him to build the synagogue he contemplated. They would even allow him to put a tower upon it. It was to be attractive—octagon-shaped, with a cupola, tower, bells, and even a striking clock. They were now not afraid of him and his ambitious plans for raising his people. The marriage of a relative in Seesen had circulated two thousand talers among the citizens. In 1805, he had received permission from the government to put up a tobacco and snuff factory in the town.[11] The school was growing too. He had started out in 1801 with three Christian and two Jewish teachers and fewer than twenty students.[12] Zincken was the principal for the first two years. The duke, informed of the school's progress through Zincken, was very sympathetic.

In May, 1802, there were forty-seven students. And now in a few years came the first graduates. What was to be done with these young folk? It was the year 1805. Jena had not been fought. The old Germany stood firm, apparently, on its rock foundations. The old disabilities, the Jewish Dark Ages, still prevailed. What could a Jew do? The pupils must learn a manual trade, decided Jacobson, the genial banker. Some had already been taught wool carding and spinning. What! Load the town with Jewish workingmen? This would never do, said the townsmen, and so it was decided that the master workmen should teach the boys unofficially, so to speak, with the understanding, of course, that none should ever practice their trade in Seesen. Jacobson was striving to educate Jews untainted by commercial pursuits, but this good man probably did not realize how little the honest burghers of Seesen really entered into the spirit of his benevolence.[13]

Jacobson lived at Brunswick where he carried on his banking business. He was very successful financially; his wealth was somewhere between a quarter of a million and a half million talers.[14] This was an enormous sum in those days and made him one of the richest Jews in the German lands. He had made his wealth lending money to the different German states. His business dealings brought him not only wealth, but also political influence and titles.[15]

In all his wealth and influence, he never forgot his people. He used his power at all times to help them. He wanted to be a leader, not among his fellow Christian-citizens, but among his own people. He loved them and wished to protect them. His loyalty to Halberstadt, the city of his youth, is characteristic. Many years after he had left her, he still continued to pay the Jewish community dues, and when the Halberstadters were in financial straits, he gave them a thousand talers additional.[16]

He boasted, and correctly, that he had not enriched himself at the cost of his fellow-citizens and the land. No one, he said, ever lost a cent through his business dealings. His banking transactions were of great benefit to the people of the Duchy. When he began his business operations, he found the rate of interest in the land had fallen to 1 percent, for there was too much idle money. Many people suffered. Widows ate up their capital; prices soared. He opened a bank, paid a fair rate of interest, and sent large sums abroad where money was scarce. Everybody benefited. To the widows and orphans, he paid a higher rate of interest; to some, he lent money without any interest whatever. Yet no one seemed to appreciate his efforts. What angered him particularly was the opposition experienced on all sides. There were circles at court that consistently opposed him. They hated him because he was successful. People refused to see what he had done for them; they only saw what he had done for himself.

Jacobson could not understand the attitude of many toward him. He had thrown himself heart and soul into the philanthropic life of the Duchy; he had given away large sums of money without regard to religion or class. He wrote that he gave 80 percent of his income to charity. This seems exaggerated, yet we know that he always lived simply and gave very freely.

Duke Charles William continued to treat him in friendly fashion, but by no means went out of his way to favor him. He gave Jacobson no titular honors.[17] Jacobson was sorely hurt by this. In 1804, on the 24th of February, the duke had naturalized Jacobson and his family.[18] The banker immediately sent in the forty-taler fee, but the Privy Council asked for an exceptional fee of 384 talers. This annoying pettiness toward one who was unquestionably the most constructive type of citizen in the Duchy was characteristic. The duke, when he heard of this chicanery, would accept no fee at all. Jaobson responded to this courtesy by sending 3,000 talers for the poor. The duke at once made it into an endowment in Jacobson's name.

But the dignified, severe justice of Charles William was not sufficient to satisfy Jacobson in Brunswick. He lived in a dream world of freedom and liberty and equality. The French Revolution was already over fifteen years old. Jacobson was tired of waiting for the millennium to come. He wanted people to think as he thought and to feel as he felt. He had traveled everywhere, he had seen much. He had no prejudices. He was willing to think new thoughts. Why could the privileged classes in the Duchy not do so too? Why could they not throw overboard their religious and social prejudices, their vested rights which limited the civil and political progress of the Jew?

Jacobson did not seem to realize that all these people had hard fought for privileges and "liberty" to lose. These rights were their life. He was gaining everything, losing nothing. It was true that he only asked for equality in the modern French sense. But this modernity of thought was impossible for men who were rooted in the past, who did not want to accept an ambitious Jew as their political equal, who felt they could not. Jacobson's disappointment can by no means be interpreted as the complaint of a disgruntled social climber. That it surely was not, for he was even now accepted by the best in society.[19]

Jacobson finally lost patience. The court cliques were stabbing him at every opportunity. His former employee, Israel Nathan, the possessor of all his trade secrets, was allowed to engage in business under the firm name of Nathan Jacob, Jr., and though he had no permission of residence, he was protected by the authorities. Jacobson's practical monopoly in banking was being taken from him. The Merchants' Guild refused to accept his son Meyer as a member despite the fact that Jacobson was a naturalized citizen and obviously entitled to all rights. The authorities were doing little to further the school at Seesen. And this school was dear to him. He took a personal interest in every child. He encouraged the teachers, he examined the children as to their scholastic progress, and even read their papers.[20]

The school was not encouraged by the state as it should have been, despite the fact that the distinguished French liberal Abbé Grégoire had visited it and praised both the school and its new principal, Bendet Schottlaender. Other schools of less importance were furthered by the state. Jacobson's request for a title for Schottlaender had been refused, but Hesse-Darmstadt had not hesitated to make Schottlaender a Hofrath. The school now cost its patron 9,000 talers a year. It had 100 children, twenty-nine of them Christians. There were eleven teachers, five Jewish, six Christian. The original purpose of providing for the children of the poor seems to have dropped out of sight. Emphasis was laid on commercial courses, music, English, French. The institution gradually assumed the character of a general elementary school.[21]

His relatives, said Jacobson, were being mistreated. The children of Herz Samson were not given the privileges promised them and were even told they could, if they wished, leave the country. As Kammeragent, he had fewer rights than in any other state. Others received pay and privileges; he, nothing. Jacobson was distraught because he was caught in the group of opposing schools of thought and because he was mentally too naive and academically too ignorant to realize his inconsistencies. He lacked an appreciation of historical change. He belonged to the nineteenth century in his insistence on equal rights for himself, for his son, for his Jewish people whose father and leader he felt himself to be. He was rooted in the seventeenth and eighteenth centuries in thinking that he had the right to monopolize the financial opportunities of Brunswick. He resented the mercantile exclusiveness of his neighbors and demanded economic freedom, yet he refused it to Israel Nathan, his former employee. When the state, pursuing its own advantage, sought to break his monopoly by encouraging Nathan, he was indignant. Jacobson was also distraught for he believed his life's work shattered. He had aimed in Brunswick to bring Jew and Gentile together. Not that he wanted to assimilate his fellow-Jews to Christianity. There was never the slightest thought of this in his mind at any hour of his career. He was a loyal Jew who wished at all times to preserve severely the religious distinctiveness of the Jew. But he assumed the existence of an implied understanding that if he would enlighten his fellow-Jews in Brunswick, then the state, in consonance with the new French liberalism, would meet him halfway. He forgot that the people of Brunswick preferred as yet to ignore the French Revolution. For them there was no implied understanding. But Jacobson did not know this. He urged his Jews to love their

Brunswick fatherland; he emphasized to his flock their obligation to the state. With his congregation he celebrated the birth of the duke's grandson.

He tried to draw his people, in their sympathies, closer to the citizens. Through his charities, which came from an honest heart, he hoped the world would realize his love for humanity and be moved to reciprocate. The culmination of untoward events now convinced him that he had failed in Brunswick, and he presented his resignation to the duke, the 8th of June, 1806. He did not want Charles William to take his side and to enter into opposition with the citizens. He wished to spare his benefactor this conflict. So he says. Actually, he realized there would be no conflict. He knew, as every one at the court knew, that the seventy-one-year-old duke, once the pride of the Prussian army, was now timid, almost craven, in the face of opposition from his aristocratic Estates.

In his letter of resignation, Jacobson was not backward in mentioning what he had done for Brunswick. Possibly he felt that the duke did not know of his services. Maybe he wanted to let the duke know what a good servant he was losing. It may even be that the resignation was a threat to bring the state to terms. His letter is filled with a strong sense of self-pity and sentimentality. Jacobson felt he had been abused. He had been, to some degree. The criticism we may direct against him is that he should have expected it. Yet his refusal to acquiesce in the shame of his time, his determination to fight for his "rights," is what makes Jacobson different from the dozens of Court Jews of his time. It is this determination that always made him a leader who would never rest until his people were accepted as full equals.

This letter of resignation, better than any other document, offers a real insight into the mind and heart of Jacobson.[22] It shows him in his forgivable weaknesses and in his admirable strength. He wrote that he was thankful for the patent of naturalization, not because of the privileges attached to it—it merely made him the equal of the least of his own Christian servants—but because it had been conferred for merit. He had cherished plans since youth to raise his crushed nation from its lowly condition. He thought that he would be able to accomplish this purpose in an enlightened state. He had worked hard to show everyone that a man could be a good Jew and a good citizen. He thought he had succeeded after twelve years in making his fellow-Jews better men. But he wanted to do more. He wanted to raise them to a high degree of culture. But, "I have lived in vain," he cried out theatrically.

This bitterness is evoked by the thought that he himself, in spite of all he had done for Jew and Gentile, was not accorded the rights due him as a citizen. He was leaving, convinced that he had done his duty, that he had furthered the fortunes of some of his fellow-citizens and dried the tears of others. He recounted in detail the successful financial operations which he had undertaken for the state. He pointed out with pride that he never resorted to usury; that no one ever lost a cent through his business dealings; that he never asked favors of the state or sought to escape taxation. Many were jealous of him, he wrote, and thought his wealth could not have been acquired honestly. They could not imagine he had made his money through hard industry. He was exasperated at the thought that, after he had succeeded honestly in ventures where others failed—and this despite the fact that all sorts of hindrances were put in his way—he was considered a dishonest fellow. He was accused of being dishonest in his business dealings. He was accused, he said, of dishonesty even to the duke, who did not seem to trust him as before. This lack of trust had been made manifest in the difficulties thrown in his way in the lottery enterprise which he saved from ruin. He knew the forces that were at work against him, but he was too proud to fight them. He could not hope for much here in this land where the people and the merchants were against him and his people.

If his rights as a citizen were not recognized, how could he hope to help his oppressed fellow-Jews who were not citizens? He wrote, rather ironically, that he was fortunate the old seventeenth-century statutes were not enforced against him to compel him to live in a Jewish quarter, for these laws had not yet been repealed. He had to leave and would leave with the feeling that even the best duke could not help a Jewish citizen. He could not stand this constant chicanery on the part of his enemies. It was embittering his life. He wound up with a tirade against his enemies. Some of them had enjoyed his favor, yet could lower themselves to defend attacks on the natural rights of man. His last message was that, though he would go, he would not rescind the charities he had devoted to the Seesen school and the Brunswick poor. The memory of his experiences at the hands of the Brunswick factions never seems to have left him. Several years later he wrote to his friend Strombeck that the mistreatment he suffered in Brunswick had almost made him misanthropic.[23]

Charles William did not want to lose his Landrabbiner and Kammeragent. He saw the justice of some of Jacobson's complaints. Still, he had not the slightest intention of limiting the vested rights of his privileged classes. So the very next day, June 9, 1806, after the receipt of the letter, he asked Jacobson what his terms were and sent his councillor, von Wolffradt, to him.

Jacobson now saw probably that he could not force his son on the Merchants' Guild. He retracted his demand[24] and accepted as compensation some commercial concessions for his sons. He asked that one of his sons be allowed to succeed him in his offices in the country. He offered to keep on hand constantly a large sum of money for state use, at 4 percent, provided he was given a premium of 1,000 talers a year. This latter offer was rejected. It is evident in the negotiations that the duke wished to retain him, but did not consider him indispensable. Jacobson, following in the footsteps of his father-in-law, had put the credit of the land on a sound basis and was no longer needed. Then, of course, there were other Jews who would gladly do his work. However, as a mark of ducal favor, he was graciously granted forage for four horses. He asked that the concessions guaranteed Herz Samson for his sons he granted them as promised and was assured that this would be done. Jacobson asked that the activity of the firm of Nathan Jacob, Jr., be stopped. The duke responded that he would legalize the residence of the interloper and later determine his exact status.

Jacobson, ever mindful of his ideals, also demanded the elimination of certain anti-Jewish laws that were out of touch with the times. The Jews were plagued and humiliated by old decrees that limited them in their business. If a Jew met a note, he had to bring the money in person to his creditor's house. Jews were also hampered in doing business at the fairs. He did not seek financial advantages for his people. On the contrary, he asked that the privilege accorded Jews of charging a 1 percent higher rate of interest be revoked. He did not want to encourage usury. He wanted his people, he said, to live according to the laws of the land, but also to be treated as equals in the courts of the land. Only in the matter of religion was the Jew to have independence. When Jews were tried in the general courts, he asked that no distinctions be made. When reports of the punishment of criminals were published, he requested that no mention of religion be made. Such things hurt the Jewish people. He was told that no change could be made in these matters until they were considered by the department that was competent to act.

Finally, he appealed for his Seesen school. He wanted it to be exempt from all taxes. Its teachers should receive recognition from the state, and only Seesen graduates ought to be employed to fill vacant pedagogic and religious offices. He hoped that those Jews who had gone to the school and learned a trade would be allowed to practice it in the Duchy. This was refused, but in lieu of it they were to be given trade concessions. Evidently the duke, like Frederick II, believed that Jews were traders and had to remain such.

Charles William, throughout this correspondence, seems to have been a consistent mercantilist. His financial agent, however, was struggling amidst a confusion of older mercantilistic and newer physiocratic and individualistic ideals in economic life which the French in the last generation had developed. He wanted the advantages of all systems. He wanted the protection which mercantilism might give to his own monopoly and he wanted the complete freedom of action for himself and his coreligionists which physiocratism encouraged. His inability to adjust himself to these conflicting ideas made him sick at heart.

Jacobson remained. He seemed to be satisfied. It is hard to see how he could have been. He had asked for much and got little, very little. It is by no means improbable that this man, keenly alive to the political problems of his day, realized that Germany was doomed at the hands of the oncoming Napoleon, and he sat back and waited.

Charles William Ferdinand probaby knew that his Kammeragent was not satisfied. He knew, too, of the petty annoyances to which Jacobson was constantly exposed by the aristocratic cliques. So it may have been at his suggestion that an unusual honor was accorded to the restless Jacobson.

On October 8, 1806, the sister of the duke, Auguste Dorothea, gave a tea to which Jacobson was invited. Auguste Dorothea respected his honest efforts "to enlighten his nation and, as far as possible, put them on an equality with the Christians." [25] She believed his deeds were guided by his "obvious vanity," yet she admired the fact that all his efforts were directed toward the raising of the people to whom he was devoted. Suddenly, to his intense surprise, two daughters of the local preacher came forward. The children advancing to honor him were meant to portray the Fatherland and the Jews joined together in friendship. The one laid an oaken crown of civic virtue on his head and the other declaimed:

> Thee, Providence has called to raise
> After a long and sorry time
> An oppressed people.
> To the deserted didst thou bring new life
> And this to do 'twas reward enow for thee.
> Thou didst see the flame quenched, O noble soul.
> Thou didst fire it mightily again to splendor new.
> What virtue, courage, work can do, thou didst show.
> Therefore accept thou now the civic wreath.

Jacobson was greatly moved and, dropping down on one knee before the princess, he pressed the garland to his breast and exclaimed: "This wreath shall some day accompany me in my coffin." Jacobson was stirred profoundly in his emotional soul. The following day the princess inspected the

Seesen school and dined there, and, a day later, she returned the compliment by inviting Jacobson and Schottlaender to her home "where we, with only nobility present, were treated to a magnificent dinner." [26]

The duke thought possibly he had now satisfied an able servant of the state who was flattered by this unusual attention. But it can hardly be questioned that an ambitious and freedom-loving man like Jacobson would not, could not, remain where a lack of liberty galled his sensitive nature. Within less than a week, the battle of Jena was fought; the age of Enlightened Despotism and the police state was past. Within a few weeks, Charles William Ferdinand died of his wounds. Jacobson was free. History was now to make the changes which the duke could not.

In the following year (1807), while still at Brunswick, Jacobson received an honorary degree of doctor from the University of Helmstedt. He knew the professors and had read and had been influenced by their writings. He loved to associate with academicians. They were flattered by the attentions of this humanitarian capitalist. They respected him for his sincere interest in the "enlightenment" of his fellow-Jews and for his generosity which recognized no religious bounds. They considered him to be an educated Jew, rather an anomaly for them. They conferred the degree, so they wrote, because he was a fine student of Hebrew literature. They dwelt on the fact that he was a friend of the arts and sciences; that he supported students and helped those in need; that he was a friend of the common good. They stressed his interest in the education of the youth, his support of the Seesen school, and his furtherance of a beneficial Enlightenment. He, thankful for the honor bestowed on him, sent the university some books and provided a place at his Seesen school for a pupil to be recommended by the university.

Goethe once referred to Jacobson as a "Jew-Savior." He was sneering from his Jovian heights at Jacobson's attempt to emancipate his people. Emancipation was a motif that ran all through the work of this Halberstadter. He wanted to emancipate the Jew not only in the state, but in Judaism also. He wanted to reform Jewry by changing its attitudes and actions. He wanted the Jew to remain loyal to his ancestral faith, but it had to be a dignified, refined faith, purified by the magic wand of rationalism. Like Mendelssohn, he wanted the Jew to be able to take his place among Gentiles as a cultural equal. Secular education would effect this change. He even hoped ultimately that the Jew might be accepted as a social equal. The political disabilities imposed upon the Jew by the Gentile world had to be removed. This was the duty of the non-Jewish world. The Jew would meet it halfway by a Jewish reform. The Jew's task in working for emancipation was a double one. He had to demand that the state free him, and he had to justify this impending political freedom through a purified Judaism. Emancipation implied for Jacobson full equality in all things. He believed that equality before the law would carry with it the acceptance of the Jew as a peer by the world about him. Jacobson wanted his Jews to be free in the fullest sense of the term, free from all pettiness, all superstition, all backwardness as he understood it. He wanted this freedom not merely for the material advantages it would bring in its wake for Jewry, but because this new change, he was convinced, was intrinsically worth while. He was not fighting for himself primarily. His political position in Brunswick, his naturalization, guaranteed to him practically all the privileges of citizenship. He was fighting for the people whose self-appointed leader he was.

Jacobson's life was devoted to this broader ideal, and all his energies were directed toward it. Viewed from this aspect, all his work is clear. He became an educator, fought for political rights, made religious reforms, all for the purpose of making the Jew a free, rational, cultured—but still distinctively Jewish—citizen. Ever since 1791, the Jews of France had civic equality. Jacobson craved this type of freedom for himself and his people. As a human being, he believed that he was entitled to share in the Rights of Man. He wanted them; he was determined to fight for them in Germany. So he went to work striving to emancipate his fellow-Jews in different German states.

Jacobson's first efforts expressed themselves in the attempt to free Jews from the unpleasant toll (Leibzoll) which was levied often in a humiliating fashion on Jewry. It was largely through his efforts, and probably through a liberal use of his own funds, that the Leibzoll was removed from the Jews of Brunswick-Wolfenbuettel and Baden in 1803 and 1804.[27] Jacobson had some contacts with the liberal Alexander I of Russia, possibly through Alexander's wife, who was a Badensian princess. Jacobson, we know, was persona grata at the Baden court, for it made him a *Hofagent* in 1803. It is not improbable that Duke Charles William Ferdinand of Brunswick, on an important diplomatic mission to Russia in 1803, may have said a good word for the Jews at the request of his agent, Jacobson. When Jacobson wrote that he had lifted up his voice before the throne of Alexander[28] and had been heard, he meant possibly that he had been of influence in the issue of the very liberal Russian "Enactment concerning the Jews" of December, 1804.

The florid poem recited in his honor in the autumn of 1806

at the home of Auguste Dorothea shows that he was recognized by his Gentile friends as an emancipator. This he had evidenced sufficiently by his educational efforts at Seesen and by his fight against the Leibzoll. This same year, in June, during his negotiations with the duke, he had besought him to do away with many old laws limiting the economic life of Brunswick Jewry.

There can hardly be any question, however, that he felt the chances for emancipation in Brunswick were slim indeed, for it was just about the time of his letter to Charles William Ferdinand that he wrote and published an appeal to Napoleon. Jacobson was a shrewd man, an international banker, in touch with the various courts of Germany, and he saw, what even a simple mind could have seen, that the future lay with Napoleon. In 1805, the French leader had sent troops into Hannover at the very doors of the Brunswick state. Troops of Baden and Hesse, of the courts where Jacobson held titles, had fought with Napoleon. Austria had been crushed in the winter of 1805. The Corsican's domination of all Germany was inevitable. His determination to dismember what was left of the mediaeval Holy Roman Empire was probably known to Jacobson.

It was in this critical period that Napoleon issued, on May 30, 1806, the decree inviting an Assembly of Jewish Notables to Paris to settle Jewish problems. Jacobson must have been mightily intrigued by this design. His letter of June to the duke showed he had no hope for the freedom of Jewry in Brunswick. He probably suspected Napoleon's new plans would affect the realm of Charles William. The impending French-controlled Confederation of the Rhine—which might even include his own Brunswick—was surely known to him. As soon as Jacobson heard in early June of the calling of the

Assembly he sent a letter to Napoleon.[29] He also sent his recently appointed Jewish school principal, Schottlaender, to Paris, to the Assembly, with a memorial urging the need for better education for Jews. In Paris, this same year, he also published in French *The First Steps of the Jewish Nation toward Happiness under the Auspices of the Great Monarch Napoleon.*[30] The book deals primarily with the Seesen school and its work. Jacobson was proud of this institution and wished to see more like it. Indeed, he felt that such an institution would help solve the Jewish problem.

We can see in this book that Jacobson looked upon Napoleon as the man who had been chosen to help the Jews. He admired Napoleon tremendously. He deplored that he had not had the good fortune to be born a Frenchman. He belonged, he tells us, to the unfortunate Jewish nation against which ignorance and superstition had banded together in order to degrade it. God had chosen Napoleon to improve this world, of which the Jews were a part. Jacobson came of the people, he says, that had suffered for a thousand years and had appealed in vain to the pity and humanity of princes. The Jews looked upon Napoleon as a savior and had found him such. Jacobson told Napoleon that he had worked for several years to improve the fortune of his nation, that he had attempted to civilize it. He had been successful. He had interested several German princes in his people and had removed the Leibzoll toll from some of them. He had established an educational institution at his own cost and had there now also twenty Christian children. But, he continued, now his hope knew no bounds in his appeal to the French Emperor. Napoleon, he prayed, would be gracious to the Jews who lived in the border lands.

The Emperor's help to the French Jews threatened to set

up a wall between them and Jews who remained in an unfavorable condition. French and German Jews maintained
close economic relations and the difference in political status
would separate the two, for the French Jew would not want
to expose himself to the humiliation that the German Jew
suffered. The status of the two groups would be so different
that French Jews would not even want to marry German
women. How fine it would be to break the bonds of an
unjustly oppressed people! The German princes themselves
would like to help their Jewish subjects. The German Jew
would consider himself fortunate if permitted to earn his
bread in an honest fashion; to enjoy the rights of citizenship. The German Jew would be happy if his religion were
to be given a post-mediaeval form; if it could be so molded
that it might be harmonized with all civil obligations—without, of course, deviating from Jewish law. Here is Jacobson's
program already clear in his mind in the year 1806. It is the
program of the "modern Jew"—the Jew who refuses to live
the life of the past cut off from the world about him. Modern
thought had so influenced him and his contemporaries that
they wanted to live the life of their neighbors whether their
fellowmen wanted them or not. They had emancipated themselves in spirit from the past. They had thrown themselves
wholeheartedly into the present. They believed that they
could be good, observant Jews and citizens of the state. Now
they wanted the state to emancipate itself from its prejudices
and accept them.[31]

Jacobson's appeal here hardly leaves much room for mis-
understanding. He knew that the Confederation of the Rhine
was on the boards, and he wanted Napoleon to grant the Jews
freedom in all those Germanic lands. He may have thought
that the new Confederation would ultimately include his own
state of Brunswick.

The most striking thought in this book is Jacobson's proposal that Napoleon organize a Jewish Supreme Council under a Patriarch with its seat in France. Larger Jewish areas were to be divided into districts; these districts were to be controlled by synods that in turn were to be under the jurisdiction of the French government and the Jewish Supreme Council. The synods would decide all religious matters and name their rabbis; the Supreme Council would have authority to give the necessary dispensations to every Jew that he might completely fulfill his duty as a citizen. This type of organization would break the political and spiritual bonds which kept the Jew enslaved. Jacobson probably meant by this that such an organization, with the French Imperial Government behind it, would have sufficient authority to assure Jewish political freedom in all French vassal states, and possibly even in the neighboring German lands. Acting as an authoritative Jewish religious body, it would have the power to change old established Jewish law so that the Jew might conform to all the demands of the modern state. After these bonds had been broken, Jacobson continues, the Jew would soon improve himself and would soon reach the same heights as his fellow-citizens. Then, he finishes grandiloquently, Jews would be able to follow in the footsteps of their fathers who had turned the barren rocks of Palestine into pleasure gardens and had planted their banners on the shores of the Jordan with the same hands that guided the plow and the weaver's spool.

The last few words are an eloquent promise. Give the Jews freedom, and they would turn farmers and learn trades and fight in Napoleon's armies. This last assurance was typical of Jacobson and his clique of enlightened autodidacts. It did not sum up the ideals of the Jewish masses of the time.

Jacobson here attempted to win the Emperor to his emancipation hopes by promising him that emancipated Jews would stop being moneylenders and take up trades. It must be borne in mind that the decree of May 30th, that year, while called together the Assembly of Notables and so stirred Jacobson legislated also against Alsatian and Rhenish Jewish moneylenders and was called to devise means whereby useful occupations might be made general among the Jews. Jacobson's book was to be an attempt to solve the Jewish problem in a manner pleasing to Napoleon and to Jews of Jacobson's complexion.[32]

The call for a Sanhedrin on September 18, 1806, to give religious sanction to the deliberations of the Assembly of Notables was probably influenced by this published appeal of Jacobson.[33]

On the 30th of November, 1807, the Prince-Primate of the Rhine Confederation issued a new decree determining the status of the Jews in Frankfort. It was called the *Neue Staettigkeit und Schutzordnung der Judenschaft zu Frankfurt am Main*. The decree was a keen disappointment to Frankfort Jewry, which had been touched by the spirit of political independence of the neighboring French lands. It was a continuation of the Middle Ages.[34] The citizens appealed to the Amsterdam community and to Israel Jacobson for help. Jacobson was now one of the most distinguished fighters for emancipation in Germany. He had won his spurs in the fight to abolish the Leibzoll, in his struggle for the establishment of modern schools, in his efforts to eliminate the old laws in Brunswick, in his fight for Jewish rights in Russia, in his interest in Jewish activities in France.[35]

Jacobson looked upon himself as the chosen leader of Jewry and was quite ready to step into the breach. Less than two months later, he published an appeal to Dalberg, the Prince-Primate, on behalf of the Jews of Frankfort. He called it, *A Most Humble Remonstrance to His Highness the Prince-Primate of the Rhine Confederation.*[36]

The spirit of the Enlightenment shines forth in every page of this appeal. The purpose of the Prince, he says, is surely to refine and to improve Jewry, a most noble purpose. He, too, Jacobson himself, has devoted his life and a large part of his fortune to this very task. Great authorities in the field of Jewish emancipation like Christian Wilhelm von Dohm and Abbé Grégoire have admitted that he has done yeoman service for his "nation," even with Napoleon and Alexander of Russia. If the Prince wishes to improve his Jewish subjects, let him allow the Jews to develop their religion and its institutions freely and completely, without hindrance, for religion is the best way to the improvement of man. But it is also a matter of reason, and no ruler has the right to command reason. Let the Jewish religion alone, and like the other religions it will develop and satisfy the demands of the state. Religion must ennoble itself. The state cannot legislate an improvement. The Protestant Consistory has no right to test the fitness of rabbis. The rabbis must retain some jurisdiction in inner Jewish life on the basis of the talmudic law. The rabbi, as a matter of fact, ought to be on the general Consistorial board to give technical, expert advice in his own field so that Jews need not be dependent on Christian officials.

Frankfort must not limit the number of her Jews. Jews develop business. The state for its own sake should encourage the admission of Jews who come with the proper credentials. Jacobson is bitter in his attack on the laws maintaining a ghetto. Conditions in Frankfort under this statute will perpetuate the Dark Ages with its barbarism. These were strong

words. He called his appeal *A Most Humble Remonstrance.*
It was anything but that. It was bold and fiery. Jacobson
was no sycophant, even though addicted to the adulatory
phraseology of his day. He did not have the ghetto fear of
the Gentile. He did not crawl. He was a man of wealth ac-
customed to association with the mighty, and courageous
because he felt his cause was just. Surely, he wrote, the Prince
cannot be serious in his decree in an age when all princes are
trying to remove the heaviest chains from the Jews. The
Prince's means of aiding the Jew (that is, through the issue
of reactionary statutes) will not work at a time when Alexander and Napoleon are encouraging them by removing
those laws which are the cause of vice and crime in Jewry.
If Jewry is bad, Christian legislation is responsible. So Jacobson believed. The laws of the Prince-Primate are harmful;
they set a bad example to others and thus hurt the Jews
everywhere. Jewish leaders who are working to improve their
own people and all peoples will surely be discouraged. If the
Prince wants to know how to help Jewry, Jacobson is at his
service.[37]

Jacobson's point of view here is obvious. It is rooted in
French and German liberalism. The Jew must have freedom
to develop; matters of conscience are inviolable; if left
unhampered the Jew will, through his leaders, work out his
own salvation to the complete satisfaction of the state. He
wanted the Jew to maintain an untrammeled religious autonomy more or less independent of the state. The Jew is a
human being entitled to equal rights with all men. Jacobson
in this writing is modern, idealistic. He is inconsistent too.
Throughout his career, Jacobson, something of a physiocrat,
encouraged the thought of a return to the soil. Here he opposed the Prince who wished for the same thing. Possibly he

saw in the suggestion of the Prince the hand of the Frankfort patricians who wanted to do away with their business
rivals. Possibly, for once, he saw that the transition from
peddling to farming had to be gradual. If he did realize this,
then it is one of the few times in Jacobson's career when he
appreciated the force of history. His appeal failed. He had
asked only what had been given to the Jews in France over
fifteen years before, but it was too much to ask of Germany.

Jacobson's bold remonstrance evoked a reply from a capable opponent.[38] His adversary, probably a Frankforter, stood
solidly on the good rights of the city to legislate for its Jews
as it saw fit. The state must interfere as far as possible for
the good of the individual. Here, strangely enough, the
German Christian approaches close to the Frederician and
Napoleonic concept of the all-sufficient wisdom of the pater-
nalistic state, while Jacobson, in his request for Jewish autonomy, is harking back to a time when all this was possible
in a decentralized, liberty-loving, mediaeval German Empire.
But the opponent, like Jacobson, forgets himself only for a
moment. The Jews are strangers in Frankfort and as such
have only those rights which history, the past, has conferred
on them. It is the historical, not the French humanitarian
attitude, that speaks here, and when in the next decade the
quarrel between Frankfort and her Jews came before the Law
Faculty of the new University of Berlin, history won, and even
Savigny voted thumbs down for the Jew. Yet all this writing
was not all loss. The problem of Jewish emancipation was
constantly pushed to the fore and became an issue in German
political life.

Goethe followed the dispute from the very beginning with
keen interest. The Frankfort Jews felt that the new decree
inspired by the jealous patricians was an attempt to crush

their economic growth. Goethe was the child of a Frankfort patrician and chuckled with satisfaction at the thought that the Frankfort literary opponent had routed the "privy-councilic Jacobinian Son of Israel." [39] Goethe did not like Jacobson, whom he considered to be a "humanity-prattler." Yet Goethe, with all his prejudices, put the problem cleverly. "It is seemly for the Brunswick Jew-Savior to consider his people as they ought to be, but one cannot blame the Prince-Primate for handling this race as it is and will remain for a while." [40]

Just about two months after Goethe's letter, on June 14, 1808, the Grand Duchy of Baden granted certain civil rights to the Jews. It is not improbable, as Kleinschmidt writes, that Jacobson's influence was present here too. He was, as we know, not without influence at this court. [41]

Jacobson was filled with a restless energy that cried out for expression. He wanted always to be doing something. His was a feverish activity. He wanted to be in the limelight. He wanted to help his people. He was not particularly successful, but no Jew of his day in Germany was more successful. The first successful emancipator in Germany was Napoleon, who represented French ideas of civil and political equality. Jacobson knew this and looked forward to political salvation from Napoleon alone. When in 1807 the new Kingdom of Westphalia, which included his Brunswick fatherland, was formed, Jacobson threw himself into the work of the new Napoleonic kingdom of Jerome, the Emperor's brother. This fullhearted support of the new Franco-German kingdom may in the eyes of some reflect on his German "patriotism." [42] Was he guilty of unpatriotic conduct? What were the circumstances that brought Jacobson into the service of the new kingdom? Charles William Ferdinand had been wounded in the battle of Jena-Auerstadt in October, 1806, and died the following month. Jacobson was no more *Landrabbiner* or *Kammer-agent*, for his appointment was binding only during the lifetime of his patron.[43] Despite the fact that the duke had never shown him more than a strict justice, Jacobson admired him and never forgot him. A few years later in the French Westphalian period, when the dynasty was outlawed, Jacobson did not hesitate to speak publicly in praise of his old patron.[44]

Jacobson did not feel the need, any more than the best minds or the most aristocratic families of the old regime, to exile himself with the Guelf dynasty, or to hesitate to work for the new French regime in Westphalia. He very probably believed—and here he stood on good German ground—that he owed no loyalty to the outlawed rulers of a defunct state which had refused to protect him from scheming intrigants. Even after Brunswick as a state was gone, during the French period, the chicanery of the Brunswick clique still continued, for a number of its members continued in power. Certain courtesies promised to his family and to his Seesen school were not granted in spite of explicit promises. He was indignant that soldiers were quartered in his Seesen school. He considered this a personal affront. He believed that he was suffering from religious discrimination.[45]

Jacobson has been accused of ingratitude for not helping Frederick William, his patron's son, who, as a fugitive from the French, wished to see him in Seesen (December 4, 1807). In this action he was joined by the aristocrats of Brunswick. For months, Brunswick had been incorporated into the Kingdom of Westphalia. To have been caught negotiating with Frederick William would have meant to jeopardize all the plans that Jacobson now had to bring about the emancipation of his people. It was probably in this very month that he was negotiating with the French authorities in Westphalia to emancipate his people by a special decree. Zimmermann tells us that he answered the young duke that he was ill and could not compromise himself. Frederick William did not take this answer amiss and prepared to transmit his messages to Jacobson through a mutual friend.[46] Schottlaender, the intimate of Jacobson, gives us a different version of the story which I find just as acceptable. Schottlaender was, I believe, a man of character. He said that Jacobson was about to help the young duke when a French officer, who had learned of the intention, intervened and threatened to shoot him if he took any action. He made Jacobson give him his word of honor not to accord any assistance to the duke. Jacobson was frightened by this threat and asked Schottlaender, the go-between, to break off all relations with the duke.[47]

Both versions of the facts show that he was guilty of no wrong. Brunswick since August, 1807, had been Westphalian. It was but natural that he should continue his activity at home. The first loyalty of every Brunswick citizen was to his state, not to the expelled dynasty. He was at least as patriotic as the best Brunswickians of his day. The best of them went into Jerome's service: von Below and even von Wolffradt, the former councillor of Charles William Ferdinand. The best families of the Westphalian lands, particularly the Brunswickians, flocked to Jerome's court and standard and were loyal to the new state.[48] The best men in Germany and German letters were happy to join his service: Johannes von Mueller, the historian, and von Dohm, the great protagonist of Jewish emancipation. But how about loyalty to Germany? There was no Germany; no "German" patriotism. That idea came to birth only through the Wars of Liberation fought against Napoleon. There was at most a Brunswick loyalty, and though Jacobson was embittered against the state, his actions toward it were always above reproach. It is true he suggested that Napoleon intervene in favor of German Jewry, but all this was done in the open, in print, and was not taken amiss by the duke or anyone else. His actions proved his patriotism. He contributed to Brunswick charities, and he represented it in the new Westphalian parliament. He was no French sycophant. He always insisted on German as the language of instruction at Seesen during the French period. He was a welcome and influential visitor in the chancellories in Mecklenburg and in Berlin during this period, and Frederick William III, almost ten years after the fall of the French, addressed Jacobson as "President," the title the French had given him.[49]

In 1807, when Brunswick became part of the new Westphalian kingdom, Jacobson was not yet forty years of age. He was in the prime of life. He was a man of fine appearance, somewhat portly, with a broad, expansive chest that strained his tightly buttoned coat. His face expressed vigor. A broad, round double chin reposing comfortably against his neck spoke eloquently of determination, energy, above all, stubbornness. The lips were broad, full, but pressed one against the other with a slight touch of a pout. The nose was straight and thin and sensitive. The eyes were wide, open, frank, lending an almost naive touch to the proud face. Curly locks nestling securely under an almost invisible skullcap completed the picture. It was the face of a fighter rather than a thinker.[50]

Yet Jacobson could think, too. Henri Stendhal knew him at this time and said that, of all his acquaintances in Brunswick, Jacobson was the only one with esprit. In addition, he said, he had all the slyness of a Jew. This was unjust. Jacobson was always frank and open. He added that Jacobson had a power-

ful Oriental imagination, that he spoke French poorly, and
that his vanity was too obvious—all of which was probably
true, but his vanity was never repulsive. Who could bear him
ill will because he gave away beautiful tobacco-boxes on
which he had put his own picture?[51] Jacobson was very
susceptible to flattery, Stendhal wrote, and if one only knew
how to get around him, he could be induced to give away
10,000 talers. In spite of this generosity, he added, he is, in
his house expenditures, stingy as a Jew. Stendhal had no understanding of a man who could possess great wealth and
could still live modestly and simply.

Jacobson was not a man of deep thoughts. His ideas were
not the result of careful consideration. He was too restless to
sit down and weigh things calmly. He had no comprehensive
sweep of problems; he merely hovered over them. He was
quick to see things, though. He had a nimble mind and his
own generation thought him talented. No fool could have
made the fortune he made in those difficult days when Jews
labored under tremendous handicaps. He was a born leader.
He was above all a brave man, never a coward. He lacked
caution; he was very often rash. He acted on the spur of the
moment. His wealth, position, and great executive powers put
him in the van of things. He was a self-made man financially
and academically. The consciousness of accomplishment filled
him with pride and gave him a very positive attitude toward
important questions. He had a great wealth of appealing
phrases and a great power of natural eloquence. He swept
young folks off their feet, though they may not have understood him—and he may not even have understood himself.
He was a fighter of dogged perseverance. He set a goal and
went after it—with a rush. He was willing to sacrifice to attain
his end. He could be witty, genial, and above all tactful. He

was always the gentleman. He never resorted to vituperation. The French courtly culture of the last two centuries had put its mark upon him. He was a businessman who had made his living at courts, and he had learned their ways. His tact was of the delicate type, and it was never better exemplified than when he sent monies to impoverished Jewish notables or struggling students. This happened very often. He made many friends and could even at times placate his enemies. He admitted that he was generous, but he was, to a fault.

He had a genuine desire to do good, and to help people. His heart really overflowed with human kindness, and when people rebuffed him or misunderstood him, he was terribly hurt. He was unduly sensitive, believing that his enemies were going out of their way to oppose him. He had a strong social consciousness and would never allow himself to be absorbed by business. People, the world, humanity, meant a great deal to him. He was in dead earnest about his work. He was a strange admixture—an idealistic, ambitious parnas of the old school shot through with modern liberalism. There was more than a touch of the Renaissance tyrant in him. His energy was almost demonic, seeking expression in every conceivable way, but always Jewish. His energy was more than his mind and body could endure. He lived more actively in a year than most men of his time lived in fifty.[52]

4.   Westphalia

The Kingdom of Westphalia, established in August, 1807, included much of the land between the Rhine and the Elbe Rivers. Brunswick was in this conglomerate of states united under Jerome Bonaparte. Jacobson was now part of a new German state under French domination.

Cassel was the capital of the new state. Why did Jacobson go to Cassel? I do not mean physically but spiritually. Cassel was the capital of the new fatherland that had swallowed up the old. He was ambitious. He always wanted to be at the scene of action that he, too, might play his part. He wanted to further himself. Influential non-Jews, knowing his abilities and ideas, invited him to come.[1]

There were financial opportunities there. But above all he saw in Cassel a chance to realize the ideals that he had cherished for many years. He saw in a French Westphalia the opportunity to bring about that reformation of his people for which he had fought in vain in Brunswick. In Cassel, he could begin work where he had been compelled to leave off in Brunswick. He had not even dared to hope for an immediate political emancipation of his fellow-Jews in Brunswick. The most he could look forward to in that place was to educate and improve his people so that the state might some day realize that they were capable of modern culture and hence worthy of political equality. This goal became the starting point in Cassel. It did not even have to be fought for. It came automatically with French occupation. The teachings of the French Revolution were on the march.

Jerome was known to be sympathetic towards the Jews. As early as September, 1807, before he even came to his new kingdom, a colored English caricature pictured him serving the far-famed Westphalia ham to eight Jews. The drawing carried the inscription: "King Jerry treating his Jewish subjects with Westphalia Venison." [2] The Westphalia constitution of November 15, 1807, in which von Dohm, the emancipator, had a voice, gave political freedom to all. [3] Jerome came to Cassel on December 10, and in a little over six weeks, on January 27, 1808, a decree was published granting equal rights to the Jews specifically. [4] To commemorate this important event, Jacobson had a medal made by the distinguished Berlin Jewish medalist, Abraham Abramson. Judaea, with her broken shackles, kneels in thanks before the altar of liberty against which the tablets of the Law rest. The inscription, in Latin, reads: "For God and the fatherly King." The reverse side disclosed two angels, Judaism and Christianity— or is it Jewry and the State?—"united in the kingdom of Westphalia." [5] Jacobson was probably instrumental in securing the passage of this decree. He was already in Cassel and in touch with the authorities. He was now considered the most distinguished Jew in the kingdom and a capitalist of repute. Jerome, the spendthrift, would need him. Jacobson was certainly elated at the turn of affairs. He had probably hoped for this, eighteen months before, as he wrote his enthusiastic *First Steps*. Now it had all come true. His sensitive soul, the soul of a "modern" man galled by living under the shadow of mediaeval disabilities—even though they were but formal in relation to him—now felt free. In Cassel, a Jew hung up a pair of shackles in his window with the legend: "Our bonds are rent asunder." [6] This was how Jacobson also felt. There were other Jews who did not lose themselves in rapture. Those close to the pulse of an unenlightened Orthodoxy did not become excited. Itzig Behrend, a contemporary, mentions the emancipation act in his diary, but without enthusiasm. [7]

Did Jacobson have a program when he came to Cassel? General ideas and hopes probably ran through his head, but there was hardly a clear-cut, definite plan. The problem for him now was to formulate a course of action that would change the life and thoughts of the Jew so as to justify the political emancipation he had already received. The modern emancipated man was a rounded out ideal in the mind of Jacobson. He was to be an intelligent, rational, patriotic, humanity-loving, moral individual. Jacobson was now prepared to devote himself to the task of raising the Jew to this ideal. He never questioned the validity of this standard, though the best minds of Christian Germany were already doing so. It never occurred to him to allow the Jew to find himself under these new conditions. But then, how could Jacobson? Even a casual knowledge of the life of the average Jew in Central Europe shows us that Jewish life had deteriorated. Something had to be done, although the situation was not so bad as the anxious Jacobson painted it. He was too impatient to let history take its course, as Goethe had suggested. But then Goethe lived, admired, in Weimar, while Jacobson's people were treated with contempt and disdain.

Jacobson wanted the Jews to be good citizens. He wanted them to become soldiers, to fight and, if need be, to die for the new fatherland that gave them the Rights of Man. He wanted them to acquire secular education, to speak a good German, to be above all reproach in their business dealings.

They must leave their peddling and enter agriculture and the industries. The people should be moral. Religious education, therefore, must be systematized and improved. The religious service must be modernized, refined. Unaesthetic superstitious customs must be thrown overboard. The community organization must be changed. These ideas ran pell-mell through his head as he sat down in Cassel in the winter and spring of 1808 to bring order out of chaos.

These ideas were not his own. They had already been discussed for a generation in Jewry. They had belonged to the period of the Enlightenment—to the preceding century. He had inherited them from Mendelssohn and his followers; from the writings of the Christian Judeophile emancipators; from his association with eminent French liberals and German thinkers. The demand for a change on the part of the Jew, an insistence that he become one with his environment, at least in externals, was characteristic of Jacobson, the Judeophiles, and even the Judeophobes.[8] But the most important fact of all was that the French government, in the flush of its revolutionary ardor, was determined not only to confer rights upon the Jew, but also to impose full civic obligations. The Jew was to be incorporated as a citizen into the new state; he was to be civilized. Modernization of the Jew was now a matter of state legislation. His changed political status was bound to affect every phase of his religious life. A harmonization of the old religion and the new citizenship was imperative.[9] Jacobson wanted this task. He was given it.

At Cassel he was accepted as the head of Westphalian Jewry. He and the French officials were evidently acquainted with the recommendations of the "Committee of Nine" of the Paris Assembly of Notables for the establishment of a French-Jewish Consistory.[10] This consistory was to organize and control Jewish life. Jacobson and the French officials planned a similar type of organization in Westphalia. The Minister of Interior and Justice, therefore, at Jacobson's suggestion, called an assembly of Westphalian Jewish notables which met on February 8, 1808.[11] The masses were suspicious of the whole proceeding, and looked askance at it. Communications had to be sent to the various communities to calm any misgivings that they might have. They were fearful of changes that might affect their religion. These communications, probably inspired by Jacobson, made clear that the notables had been called together to teach the citizens a proper conception of their civil duties. This assembly was, furthermore, to decide how present Jewish custom which was not essential to the religion might be so modified as to bring Christian and Jewish fellow-citizens closer together. This was necessary because of their community of political interests. In no wise, however, was the Mosaic law to be touched. This was made clear.[12]

The Westphalian Jewish Notables assembled on February 8, 1808,[13] almost a year to the day since the similar French Sanhedrin had met. Jacobson was the guiding and dominant spirit in all that was said and done. Nothing was attempted without his approval. The delegates were introduced the following day to the king. Jacobson spoke. He was always ready to speak. He told Jerome that throughout the kingdom, before his arrival, the Israelites had suffered under a barbaric system of laws. But now, all that was over. The Jew was a citizen and would furnish the armies with soldiers, the fields with peasants, and the cities with merchants. He meant what he said, but he did not seem to realize that he was not speaking for even 5 percent of the kingdom's 16,000 Jews[14] who eked out a bare existence at best, and were more worried about the obligations of citizenship than its privileges. A committee was appointed at the suggestion of Jacobson to consider how to establish a synagogal service that would satisfy the religious law, yet would not require the retention of all the old customs. The delegates adopted resolutions recommending that all disorder during the service be avoided; that the proper solemnity prevail, and that the essential be separated from the unessential.

The consistory was to compose a proper catechism, and every teacher appointed was to employ it and no other. The teacher was strictly forbidden to insinuate his own ideas into his instruction. Before this catechism should be promulgated it was to be respectfully submitted to the state authorities. The control of the Jewish poor from now on should be turned over to the local police in order that the Jewish communities in the future should not be held responsible for the crimes of Jewish beggars and idlers.

There was quite a bit of discussion on the matter of marriage and divorce. All Jews insisted that though the civil act of marriage or divorce may precede, the religious act must not be omitted. Some even asked that a religious action should precede the civil, but to this the state would not agree. The conservative character of the delegates comes strongly to the fore here. The general rule was finally adopted that all laws in conflict with the Code of Napoleon were to be dropped, inasmuch as other religions also accommodated themselves. Jacobson reported on the academic requirements necessary for rabbis and teachers. It was decided that a rabbi had, at least, to know the *Shulchan Aruk*, Hebrew well enough to teach it, and German enough to be able to preach on moral problems. The government was asked by the Assembly that rabbis be given the privilege of censoring Jewish books, whether in Hebrew or in German. Jacobson also reported on the committee that formulated the general character of the consistorial work. He declared that there were three types of commandments in Judaism: the fundamental principles, which were inviolable; the moral laws, which were closely related to the religion; and finally the various Mosaic commands and prohibitions. The Consistory had no authority to touch the first two groups of teachings in Judaism. It was to have the right to exercise its discretion with respect to the last group.[15]

The report handed in to Minister Siméon on February 26, 1808, summed up the decisions made by the delegates. They hoped that they had surmounted the difficulties so that the religious laws and the state laws had been harmonized, and a closer approach of the Jews and the Christians effected. They promised that a more refined generation, improved through a better education, would know how to merit the rights of citizenship with which it had been blessed. The consistory reserved the right to alter customs that had crept in, so that there might be an adjustment with the spirit of the times. Of course, when such changes were made, His Excellency would always be informed. The phrases employed by this assembly are interesting. They speak of "all types of manual trades and completely useful citizens"; "the patriotic confessors of the Mosaic Law"; "that the coming together with believers in other religions be furthered"; "from the institutions of education men will go forth worthy to serve the state to which the [Jewish] nation owes so very much"; "the enlightenment of the mind"; "the spread of religious morality"; "leading the new citizens to moral tendencies." A number of these phrases are catchwords of the Enlightenment.

Jacobson's letter to Minister Siméon submitting this report

is eloquent: "I further flatter myself, Monsieur, that you will be convinced by this report that the Israelites wish truly at heart to be useful to the state, and that they have united all their efforts to attain this purpose." [16]

In this new French-controlled land, the consistorial form of government for Jewish affairs was inevitable. Jacobson did not create it and is not responsible for all its errors and faults. The French employed the consistorial form of control for religious bodies because it permitted the state to dominate them. It was a historical accident that Jacobson was chosen to lead this Jewish consistory. A working adjustment between synagogue and state was inevitable. He was responsible only for those changes which were made at his initiative. His note stated clearly that the purpose of the changes proposed at this initial conference was to make the Jews "useful to the State." It would be unjust to Jacobson here to take him at his own word. In his answer to the French, he mentioned only that phase of the work which he knew would interest them. Personally he was deeply interested in all the proposed reforms. He had contemplated and preached some of them for several years. He honestly believed that Judaism could live in a modern environment only through change, so as to meet with the spirit of the time. But his interests were not primarily religious. He did not wish to effect those religious reforms for the sake of religion itself. He honestly and truly wanted to make the Jew presentable in his cultural and social and religious acts. He had no inner spiritual compulsion to be a religious reformer. Throughout this conference at Cassel, it is the emancipator who speaks, the emancipator in the broadest sense.

The views recorded at the assembly were not really the members', but Jacobson's and his group of helpers. His

opinions were not representative of the delegates, who came to
life only when they protested—in vain—against the all-suf-
ficiency of the state in the matter of marriage and divorce.
It is the old parnas who is always speaking here, albeit an
enlightened one. Westphalian Jewry, which had lived under
the heavy hand of a number of Court Jews and community
chiefs for years,[17] had merely changed to the control of one
who was modern and a gentleman, but just as insistent on
carrying through his ideas and just as prepared to employ
force. There had simply been a change of masters, a change
from petty autocracy to a benevolent despotism.

Jacobson at this assembly left no doubt as to what he
wanted and what he was willing to pay for it. Because he had
received the full rights of citizenship he was ready to sacrifice
the remnants of cultural autonomy and was prepared to sub-
mit to the state in almost anything except what he considered
to be the fundamental principles of religion. In the enthusiasm
of the moment, he probably promised more than he could,
emotionally, as a Jew perform. In practice and in emotion,
he was attracted to the old customs in which he had grown
up. In theory, he was dominated by the unhistorical, pale
liberalism of the Enlightenment. Jacobson was never a strong
enough intellect or a sufficiently keen thinker to wipe away
the love for the old or to effect a working harmony of the
two. He always spoke liberally and for his time radically, but
he thought and often felt like an old-fashioned Jew. Years
later, in Berlin, he is reported to have said to some old
friend: "My happiest days were spent in Halberstadt. In
what an exalted, delighted mood was I then when I recited
in the synagogue the blessings for dew and rain!"[18]

In the synagogue at Cassel, on the 11th of February, 1808,
a service was held to give thanks for the rights of citizenship

formally conferred on the Jews on the 27th of January. Jacobson preached in German: Fear the Eternal and the King.[19] At this service he made a public contribution of 3,000 francs on behalf of the deputies "for our poor brothers no matter what religion they may profess." [20] A broad, universalistic spirit always moved Jacobson in his charities. The educated Jews of Westphalia, under the influence of liberal teachings, felt that a new day was dawning in which all prejudice would be wiped out. The non-Jews there were so busy adjusting themselves to the French that they had no time to think about the Jews, let alone dislike them, and so the Jews really believed that a change had come about for the better in intergroup relations.

Jacobson was president of the commission to work out a sketch for a consistory. On the 31st of March, 1808, the consistory was established.[21] It followed closely the French consistory decree that had been published just two weeks before. It copied it verbatim in certain matters. An important difference was that this consistory allowed for a layman as leader; in France, the rabbis were the chiefs. This provision was made to assure the leadership to the ambitious Jacobson. The decree made it perfectly clear that the Jews must not in the future be a separate group in the state, but, like the other religions, must assimilate to the secular nation of which they are a part. The selfish attitude of the state during this process of reorganization was most clearly evinced in the bald statement that the rabbis and schoolteachers must at every opportunity cultivate loyalty to the laws and especially to those which refer to the defense of the fatherland. They must in their instruction represent military service as a holy duty during the performance of which the Jewish law frees man from all religious customs in conflict with his civil duties.

No sooner was the decree published than the people were disturbed by it. Every effort was made to calm them and to make them understand that it was for their good. Schott (Schottlaender), the principal of Jacobson's school at Seesen, now issued a call to the people to support the consistory.[22] In this appeal written, without doubt, at his patron's suggestion, he laid down a program which represented the aims of Jacobson. Schott was well-read in the Enlightenment philosophers. Their ideas had become part of his intellectual makeup. So it is an eighteenth-century rationalist and deist who is speaking here to thousands of simple Jews whose intellectual background lay in the talmudic and mediaeval ages. I can well believe that his appeal did little to calm or reassure the Jews that no important changes were contemplated in their religious life and organization.

He at once made a distinction between the spiritual and the sensual in religion. Ceremony in itself might be of importance to clarify religious thought, but it was not religious in itself. These ceremonies could be modified. It would be the function of the consistory to institute a suitable religious service and to study all laws and customs now in vogue in relation to their capacity to promote true devotion. What was harmful to true worship would be removed. The religious service would be simplified. New customs would be introduced to revive the old religious feeling. Spiritual hymns would be sung to encourage religious sentiment. Schools would be established to educate religious teachers. Yes, even inner religious changes would be made, although all this was to be done carefully so as not to encourage doubts and indifferentism. Uncalled for new ideas would not be tolerated. Yet all wrong ideas had to be fought. Even the rabbis of old had not hesitated to change the biblical laws of marriage and calendation. All that hurt true morality, the interests of humanity at large, and all that impaired the obligations of citizenship would be opposed. Even though some of the teachings that stood in the way of these ideals were old, they had to be changed. Religion was the most important thing in life. The implication here was that, since it was so, the consistory had the right to take radical action to control it, to improve it. Just about this time, Jacobson published his *Humble Remonstrance* on behalf of the Frankfort Jews. Here, too, he emphasized the importance of religion for Jewry and forbade the Christians of Frankfort to interfere in such a sacred issue. Jacobson told the Prince-Primate there that the Jewish religion could develop into a faith that would satisfy all the requirements of the state if the state did not interfere. The state was wrong in seeking to ennoble religion. Religion had to do this for itself.[23] Hands off! In Westphalia, Jacobson, Schott, and their associates did just what they had adjured the Christians of Frankfort not to do.

Jacobson, said Schott in his declaration, would have only good men on the Consistorial Board. But Schott said nothing of their scholarship or Orthodoxy. The value of this consistory would be to bring unity into the Jewish religion. This unity would make development and accomplishment easier. Now a better religious training was to be possible after the slumber of centuries. Education would improve the ritual laws and external observances. An ideal of Jewish education was mirrored in the lives of the Patriarchs, those models of virtue who lived in the bosom of mother nature. Their teachings were recorded in the Bible, the most complete system of morals that men possessed. Here Rousseau spoke through the mouth of Schott. But, alas, Schott went on, contemporary Jews were different from the ideal Patriarchs of old. They were in a sorry condition because of superstition and ignorance on the one hand and infidelity and scoffing on the other. It weakened religion for people to pray in a language which they did not understand. To prove this, Schott quoted the talmudic statement that the *Shema* may be recited in the vernacular. His people no longer understood the Bible. They did not care for true religion. The education of Jewish women was being neglected, and so they turned to trashy novels which stimulated the physical senses and the powers of fantasy. Schott was as indignant with the Jewish radicals as he was with the unyielding Orthodox. There were too many false enlighteners who set fire to a shrine and thought they had made light. Poor education here, too, was the cause of scorn and unbelief. A good education had to affect the heart and mind. Unless customs in religion were explained and understood, they only served to further mechanical observance of the ceremonial law. The new consistory would teach a true religion, a trust in God and His commandments. Citizenship would bring about a new golden age, and Jews were no more to be isolated from Christians. By supporting the consistory, Jews could show that they appreciated the goodness of the king, who had done more for them than his German predecessors. All this was the battle cry of Schott and Jacobson. But Jacobson soon found out that it was easier to formulate programs than to carry them out.

Now that the consistory had been established, the problem was, of course, to perfect a working organization. Jacobson knew that big things were in the making and proceeded to ask advice of important individuals, Jews and Christians, liberals and conservatives. Heinemann, his secretary, gives us the impression that Jacobson was for radical measures, but was dissuaded by his friends from going too far. These sessions of the Assembly which he dominated show that he would have had no hesitation in altering the ceremonial law if he had thought it necessary. He corresponded with Friedlaender, Wolfssohn,[24] Herz Homberg, Peter Beer and Benzeeb, all Mendelssohnians and known radicals, but he wrote also to Lazarus Riesser, who counselled moderation.[25] Among the Christians, he appealed to the Abbot Henke, the famous church historian, and Chancellor Niemeyer of Halle, the theologian. Henke, a personal friend, believed that religions had to be freed from the debris of the centuries. Niemeyer was interested in the improvement of religious instruction.

Friedlaender made a strong effort to make Jacobson see things the way he saw them. Aaron Wolfssohn, the principal of the Jewish school in Breslau, came down to see Jacobson and talk over things with him at the suggestion of Friedlaender, who was indignant that all Jacobson contemplated was the omission of a few mishnaic passages from the liturgy. Either attack the problem boldly and change everything, or let the structure decay and rot. No man of intellect would join himself to the spiritual leaders Jacobson had picked for the consistory. Friedlaender had evidently heard that Jacobson was choosing conservative rabbis for the Consistorial Board. Friedlaender did not think that the younger men about Jacobson—he meant Fraenkel and Heinemann—could do much because they would not dare oppose the rabbis or possibly they, too, still believed in the infallibility of the Talmud and in the milk and meat laws. Friedlaender wrote Wolfssohn to urge Jacobson to make no compromise with old ideas and to spare nothing.[26]

The radicals did not accomplish anything. Jacobson probably inclined more towards the Left than the Right, but he did not want to break with the Orthodox. There were too many threads tying him to the past. He loved the old Judaism too much to make the break. Conversation, too, with Orthodox leaders warned him that the Jews would bitterly resent any radical departures.[27] He saw that there would have to be a gradual development.[28]

Jacobson's determination to make haste slowly was shown quite obviously by the staff he picked to help him. Though appointed by the state, they were in reality his nominees.[29] He had appointed Rabbis Loeb Mayer Berlin, Simon Kalkar, and Mendel Steinhardt as Clerical Councillors.[30] David Fraenkel, school principal and editor, and Jérôme Heinemann were appointed Lay Councillors. Merkel, a Christian attorney, was appointed secretary. It was a compromise cabinet. Berlin, an old, respected rabbi, came of a family of Court Jews. Though a mild liberal, he was by no means a reformer, and he was not under the thumb of Jacobson.[31] Steinhardt and Kalkar were both, like Berlin, Orthodox Jews. Berlin and Steinhardt were not untouched by the newer education, and Steinhardt was sympathetic to ritual reforms.[32] Heinemann, Jacobson's secretary, seems to have been a moderate liberal, at least in Westphalia, in the days of Jacobson. Fraenkel, judging from his writing, was a radical, and a strong influence on Jacobson.[33]

On October 2, 1808, in a letter to Minister Siméon, Jacobson proposed the names of his associates. He admitted that they would not satisfy the enlightened, implying by this that they were a little too conservative for him. But they were moral and willing to dedicate themselves to helpful reforms and pursue enlightenment. One of the chief reasons for which he had selected these men was to convince the reactionaries, those who would hold tight to the old dogmas, that he had noble motives and did not wish to make changes merely for the sake of change. These men would do their best to harmonize the civil with the religious obligations. In this same letter, he specified as the chief immediate cultural duties of the consistory: child education and the regulation of the religious ritual. Jacobson evidently felt that the chief work of his consistory would be along educational lines.[34]

That same month the seal of the consistory was adopted. It was called the Royal Westphalian Consistory of the Mosaic Religion.[35] In the same letter, he asked permission to wear, as president, a black robe with silver embroidery, and the Ten Commandments around his neck. This was the first costume of the modern Jewish religious leader.[36] Jacobson took the oath with covered head, and on the 19th of December the consistory was formally opened.

Jacobson's address at the opening of the consistory showed how his program was shaping itself. To succeed, he said, we must be supported by a higher religious sense and an ardent, inner love for our coreligionists. He pointed out that the work of the consistory would not be that of mere control of already established institutions; it would require constructive leadership. The form of the religious service, the synagogal institutions, and the religious, scientific, and civil education of the Jewish youth were not such that all the consistory needed to do was maintain them as they were or make slight changes. No. Jews were sadly deficient in fundamentals. Everywhere Jewish life showed a contrast, an unfavorable one, with the culture of the century. One would meet on all sides things that had for a long time demanded improvement, and against which prominent Israelites had in the past cried out. Jewry's bad condition was due primarily to the bad laws of the states. Yet the character of Jewry's divine religion and the living feeling for it have always maintained themselves among the larger number of Jacobson's coreligionists. Now, with the happy rebirth of the Mosaites these defects could not be tolerated if Jews wanted to maintain the confidence of the king.

The truly religious feelings of most Jews—and the best of them—had to strengthen the consistory and help it to attain success. The consistory was not only against that bigotry which held equal the kernel and the shell; it was also against that false enlightenment which threw away the kernel with the shell. But the truly religious would know how to separate the one from the other and gladly modify nonessential institutions and customs as soon as the purified reason realized that these were useless or harmful. It would require courage to uncover all that was defective in organized Jewish life and in the Jewish school system, but through firmness the consistory had to get rid of the weeds in the garden of God and put better plants in their place. The consistory had to do what it could to establish laws so that Jewish youth would be prepared for the high destiny of citizens and family heads. A church discipline had to be established that would accord with the old, divine Jewish religion and with the position now assured Jews among their Christian fellow-citizens. The motto of the group would be to love the truth, to wish the good, and to do the best. He proposed finally in this address that a plan for the church constitution and the school system be worked out to lay before the authorities.

What Jacobson was working for was evident here in this programmatic address. He was not going to maintain conditions as he found them and merely make his consistory a supervisory body. He intended to make changes along ritual and educational lines in order the better to fit the Jew into his new environment of citizenship. Jacobson was concerned, very much so, as to what the Christians thought of the Jews. He evidently felt that the religion itself required no reforms. He wanted merely to remove the wrappings that obscured the pristine pure faith. It was Rousseauan romanticism that moved him here, French and English deism that demanded a return to a pure religion of the past. He intended steering a path between the conservatives and the radicals. He did not seem to realize that those who sympathized with him were indeed few. The great majority of the people were very conservative and were "very much attached to the old dogmas."

The function of the consistory was really an all-embracing one. It set about to improve not merely the religion but also the secular life of the Jews.[37] The transformation of Jewish life attempted by Jacobson was to be accomplished through the medium of a series of laws and decrees. On the 15th of March, 1809, the important *Duties of the Rabbis* was published. In the welter of detail, we are told that rabbis must live morally and that they must edify their communities occasionally through sermons in German, if possible. Now and then these addresses must be forwarded to the consistory. They are to encourage obedience to the laws, especially those that deal with the defense of the land. This thought is emphasized, too, in the oath that the consistory members must take. Military service is a holy duty, and during its practice all Jewish laws that cannot be reconciled with it need not be enforced. Prayers for the king are to be recited. These specific patriotic instructions are to be found also in the older French Consistorial decree.[38] The vital statistics are also to be maintained by the rabbi. This, of course, is necessary for the conscription records. The rabbi must seek to prevent everything that disturbs the devotions in the synagogue or creates an alarm there. He must prepare the youth for confirmation and teach the aspirants himself. He is to inform the consistorial authorities about those brilliant students who should be encouraged to seek higher education. The rabbi is to receive no perquisites directly. He is not to engage in trade or a secular occupation. He must not allow dissension with other religions, for all faiths which honor an Eternal Being are in reality sisters; all people are children of one Father.

There is hardly any question that most of the laws in the French decree establishing the consistory and setting forth the duties of the rabbis as agents of the state were dictated by the Napoleonic government, which made the same demands of the Catholics and the Protestants. These laws were to be found also in this Westphalian *Duties of the Rabbis.* But this decree made by Jacobson went farther. The thorough surveillance over almost every act of the rabbi, his complete subordination to the consistory, was a layman's touch—again the touch of the old parnas spirit, the despotism of the Court Jew. Jacobson, because he was a layman and had no real understanding of the spirit of the rabbinate, broke with all its finest traditions. He had no real understanding of or sympathy for it and standardized the rabbi down to the level of the village preacher. The humanitarian and universal enthusiasm, the swooning affection for all peoples—these were all his own. That same day the *Duties of the Israelitish Syndics* was issued also at Cassel. In this instruction, which informed the communal leaders how they were to govern and what was expected of them, they were also told that "the purpose of all our institutions is to make those Israelites who are not yet what they ought to be, worthy respecters of their holy religion, true subjects of the government, and moral men." In general, in this decree, emphasis was laid on moral living. Evidently, Jacobson felt that the moral life of the village Jew left much to be desired. He betrayed that faint touch of righteous satisfaction which usually characterizes the philanthropic Jew in his relation to his less fortunate and less cultivated coreligionists.[39]

To explain further to the state the activities of the consistory, Jacobson submitted a memorial, a survey touching briefly on the history of the preceding thirty years. He pointed out the bad state of education among the Jews of Germany. He spoke of the petty traders who knew only the Talmud and observed rigorously the letter of the ceremonies. Then, he said, came Mendelssohn, the first to further education. After him came the Enlightened, but they were opposed by the Orthodox (*Stockjuden*). A struggle arose, and some of the Enlightened drifted away from the faith as a result of this quarrel. It is evident that Jacobson here took a middle place between these two groups. The laws of the lands did not give the Jew a chance to develop himself. The Prussian state wanted to further education and agriculture, but the rabbis were in opposition. In larger cities, after the death of the old-fashioned rabbi, no new one was appointed. Thus politically, religiously, culturally, economically, educationally there was a crisis in Jewish affairs, and this continued down till the establishment of the Kingdom of Westphalia. France, of course, had given the Jews civil equality years ago, but no change was made in the religious organization. None had been thought necessary. This was a mistake. Jacobson wrote to Napoleon, and the Emperor, Jacobson says, heeded his words.[40] But the carrying out of these ideas of Jewish organization had been more successful in Westphalia. Jacobson wished to show the importance of the Westphalian Jewish Consistory as a pioneer in the work of assimilating the Jew to

the national state. Jacobson implied here that the problem of
the Westphalian Consistory was to adjust the entire Jewish
life of yesterday to the new world into which it now had to
enter, the world of civil emancipation.[41]

Through the personality of Jacobson the consistory was a
living organization striving to remold Jewry in Westphalia
after the image of its president. The French consistory limited
itself to religious administration and made few changes beyond those required by the authorities. Jacobson, however,
attempted completely to reorganize life in his land. The consistory fought to remove all disabilities imposed on Westphalian Jews who visited other states. It tried to protect Jews
from being called to court on Jewish holidays. Jacobson attacked the ignoble form of oath that Jews were compelled
to take in court.[42] He was willing to establish a Jewish or-
phan home, but refused as a matter of principle to help the
Jewish poor and ailing, for he and the consistory did not desire to emphasize the disparateness of Jew and Christian.
General communal responsibility for all the sick would help
to bring the two religious parties closer to one another and
would cause religious hatred to give way gradually to the
sentiments of human tenderness. The consistory, in its efforts
to industrialize the Jew, helped poor Jewish youths to become
painters, tailors, shoemakers, saddlers, and the like. This effort
was in line with the general program of the state which fought
pauperism through teaching children a trade. Here Jacobson
and his council were emancipators and dictators of folk-
policy.[43]

It is not strange, therefore, that in the order of his duties
Jacobson exerted himself to free Jewish prisoners and criminals from working on the Sabbath and holidays. The consistory made this request of the Minister of the Interior on

April 17, 1810. This, they said, would be a violation of conscience. The Minister declined to accede, protesting that discipline in the institutions would not permit such exceptions. If this were permitted the men would also ask for special food. The Minister, von Wolffradt, slyly added that Jacobson would not want this since he wished to remove all differences between the religions. This rather embarrassed Jacobson. He did preach sometimes the wiping away of religious differences. He meant it when he said it, particularly if there were plenty of Christians in the audience to spur him on.

What he did not seem to realize quite clearly was that, through his early training and his emotional urges, he was very much a particularistic Jew enjoying the ceremonials and the observances of his fathers and his own youth. Jacobson was in a quandary, for von Wolffradt had asked him to make suggestions in this matter. If he recommended that the prisoners be allowed to observe the holidays, he would be opposing the best interests of the state whose official he was. Yet he was also an official of the Jewish consistory and did have strong Jewish loyalties. Where did his prime loyalty lie? The problem was clear-cut. Jacobson's answer is important. He avoided the problem. He sent his Confession of Faith to the Minister and asked the Minister to read it and to determine from it what should be done.[44] Jacobson did not insist, as he might well have done, that Jewish prisoners be given specific religious rights. He was too new a citizen. Unconsciously he felt that citizenship was a conferred gift and that Jewry would do well not to insist on its rights. In the inevitable conflict between State and Church, he did not wish to antagonize the state to which his people owed so much, yet he did not think of completely surrendering the Church in this matter to the State. He lived in a transitional age, between a mediaeval autonomous Jewry and a modern enfranchised Jewry in the secular state, and hence was torn between two emotions.

A feeling of solidarity with Jewry everywhere always filled Jacobson's heart. His "love for his coreligionists," he told the Prussian minister, Hardenberg, was a "passion" with him.[45] He wanted to help emancipate Jewry in Mecklenburg and Prussia and applied his not inconsiderable influence to this purpose. He was one of the three or four leading Jews of Germany who interceded with the Prussian authorities. Prussian Jewry was now, through its leaders, moving heaven and earth to attain the rights of citizenship. Jacobson wrote to Hardenberg appealing for his aid. They had been friends for twenty-five years, for the Prussian statesman had served, like Jacobson, under Duke Charles William Ferdinand. It is by no means improbable that Hardenberg was indebted to Jacobson and his family for past favors and wished to show his gratitude by being sympathetic to Jewry. This was not a difficult task for him. He was a liberal and not averse to Jewish emancipation.[46] Jacobson asked Hardenberg to help because it would not only improve the position of the Jews themselves, but would also further the welfare of the state. He could not imagine, he said, how the liberal Prussian state had remained behind in the work of regenerating the Israelites.[47]

The day after he wrote to Hardenberg, Jacobson wrote also to Sack, one of the most important officials in the Prussian bureaucracy. Jacobson had already seen Sack and he repeated in writing what he had said orally. It is a strong letter and shows Jacobson, the belligerent emancipator, at his best. Jacobson, as in his letter to Hardenberg, could be flowery and complimentary and even sentimental, but he was never servile. His letter to Sack is vigorous. Nothing but antiquated religious prejudices or the weakness or suspicions of the government stood in the way of making his coreligionists citizens with all rights and duties. The Jews could develop, if they were given opportunity. Man was capable of attaining perfection. Again it is the voice of Rousseau speaking. The rights which had been taken from the Jews had to be first returned to them; then one might seek to solve those problems in Jewish life caused by the prejudices of the time or a neglected education. It was sophistical to object to the Jews because of some detail in the Talmud or the delinquency of Jewish criminals. Westphalia was the proof that a liberal policy would accomplish much. Religion, humanity, and cleverness demanded that, if the state did not wish to harm itself, if it did not wish to be inconsistent, it had to show confidence in, and love and respect for its native Israelites as for all other citizens.

The state had no right to interfere in a man's inner transformation, particularly in a land like Prussia, which looked upon freedom of conscience as one of her most treasured possessions. This inner change would come of itself after the emancipation, through the help of the proper leaders in Prussia. Jacobson, no doubt, had in mind men like Friedlaender and his associates. To show Sack how things were being done in Westphalia, he sent him a number of the decrees of the consistory to prove to him how Jews there were freeing their minds of prejudice, warming their hearts for love of mankind, and winning souls for everything good and noble. If he had been indiscreet, he added in his last paragraph, he asked to be pardoned, for the emancipation of Jewry was his favorite theme for which he would spare no expense or mental effort.[48] Jacobson's intervention was not without success. Sack wrote to Hardenberg of Jacobson's appeal and asked for some sort of decision in the matter.[49]

The following month found Jacobson busy in Mecklenburg-Schwerin on behalf of the Jews. Jacobson had a great deal of influence in that Duchy. As early as 1806, he had been made a Privy Finance-Councillor. His business relations there were very intimate. He had an interview with Frederick Francis, and on the 17th of March, while still in the capital, Schwerin, he wrote a formal letter to the duke. He pleaded that the Jews be freed. Religion did not impair good citizenship, oppression did. As in his argument in Prussia, here, too, he pointed with pride to the accomplishments of Jewish citizens in Westphalia. The Israelitish citizens there were working for the state and had become scholars, artists, soldiers, artisans, and statesmen. The very next day, the 18th of March, the duke answered from Ludwigslust. He expressed most cordially his sympathy with Jewish emancipation and said that he was considering the matter very carefully with the Estates. He meant it, too, for on February 22, 1813, Mecklenburg-Schwerin Jewry was emancipated.[50]

The object of the consistory was, we have said, to adjust the Jew completely to the new age with its new opportunities and new responsibilities. This meant, politically, to maintain newly acquired rights and to extend them if incomplete. But there were really no political difficulties for Jacobson in Westphalia herself. There was, however, the problem of adjusting the Jew mentally and intellectually and culturally to his environment. Jacobson felt that this could best be done through the school, through education. Here the child could be educated properly to be a man, an Israelite, and a citizen. Here poor children could be prepared for agriculture and the army, and thus be really useful. Here the teachers, through their religious and moral instruction, could lay the proper emphasis on humanitarian and civil obligations.[51] He did not care to found his new Jewish life on a Jewish ethic. He may have felt such an ethic too narrowing, not sufficiently humanitarian. He was always convinced of the supreme importance of the school. He had felt this several years back when he founded the school at Seesen. The idea of working through the schools, through the impressionable young rather than the immovable older generation, was not new. The plan of solving all inner Jewish problems by capturing the Jewish youth was the dream of the whole post-Mendelssohnian school in the years after the sage's death. They believed conditions to be bad. They were bad. There were no competent teachers or rabbis who understood the difficulties of the age. The rabbis, mostly of the old school, ignorant of the language of the land, fearful of the new world about them, opposed all change for the better. The yeshiboth were deserted; many rabbinical positions were left unfilled; instructors in the villages were hopelessly incompetent. As a matter of fact, there was a new age dawning for which no adequate system of education had been established. The old world of Yiddish, gemara, cabala, and the *derashah* (the old-fashioned homily) was dead. The world of German, rationalism, and modernity had been born.

Wessely, Mendelssohn, Beer, and a host of others had fought for better instruction in the schools. In this group of educators, there was no more outstanding figure than Jacobson in the first decade of the nineteenth century. Jacobson wanted secular and religious education in the Jewish schools of the new kingdom. He did not wish, however, to separate the secular from the religious training in the larger Jewish communities, to send the child to a non-Jewish school for his elementary secular training. All Jews, even radicals like

Friedlaender, were in sympathy with the Jewish communal school.[52] Secular education, they felt, would bring the Jew closer to the times and the non-Jews. Religious education of the proper type would not only prove to the non-Jew that Judaism was a worthwhile faith, but would give the Jew a truer appreciation of the inner beauties of his ancestral religion. The work of raising the religious level of the Jew and purifying Judaism from the accretions of the centuries could be done only through schools and would involve the training of the proper teachers and rabbis and the correction of faults in Jewish ceremonial life, in the home and the synagogue.

Jacobson's religio-educational program was thus clearly laid out before him. He and his clique conceived of education and schools as their most important undertaking, their most effective instrument. One of the first official pronouncements of the consistory was that it would busy itself with modern educational institutions and through them seek to do away with the confusion and even improprieties that had been tolerated before this time.[53] A public school for boys was set up in Cassel, and various elementary schools were furthered and encouraged throughout the country.[54]

A seminary for teachers and rabbis was founded.[55] The official announcement that preceded the establishment of the seminary made it clear that, through good teachers and rabbis, the danger of the disappearance of true religiousness would be avoided and truly religious rabbis would be educated. The prejudice of Jacobson and his group against the rabbis of the old school was never hidden. Members of the consistory traveled about everywhere to assist the educational work. In a memorial to the Minister of the Interior, von Wolffradt, the wishes of the consistory in the matter of Jewish education for teachers and rabbis were set forth. Hebrew and history were to be the beginning disciplines. Aramaic was necessary for reading the Talmud and its commentaries. There was not the slightest breath of disagreement with the Talmud as such, although frequent references were made to "true religion" in contradistinction to ceremonial in religion. The curriculum of the seminary would include, besides the Bible, the Talmud and talmudic literature, the code of Maimonides and other halachic codes, theology on the basis of the Pentateuch, oratory, and composition. The morality of the student would be carefully observed. But the secular education of the rabbi, too, was to leave nothing to be desired. Because he had lost the jurisdiction and power that he possessed under the old system of autonomy, he had to be compensated at least by being accorded the same rights as all other clergymen. He had to work to improve the moral and civil status of his flock and evidence true religiosity, not through rigorous practice of the ceremonial law, but through the maintenance of a pure morality and an unspotted character.

The hope was also expressed that graduates of the seminary would be sent beyond the confines of the land to help Jews everywhere. It was intended that all appointments of rabbis and teachers be made through the consistory. Rigorous and centralized as the French Consistorial Board was, it was in general more liberal than the Westphalian consistory which made Jacobson absolute in authority. He wanted to centralize all power in his person because he felt that he could do the work best and because he felt that a firm and unified control was beneficial and efficient. But he was not a harsh man. In his personal relations with everyone, he was a lovable, charming man whose sincerity of intention and innate goodness of heart were acknowledged even by his enemies. Jost,

the historian, who knew him intimately, wrote of him as a
man in the highest terms.[56]

The consistorial school was one of the first public schools
in Germany. A modest fee was levied, but arrangements were
made to educate fifty poor boys free of charge. Twenty-five
of these were to be taught trades, fifteen the sciences and
business, and ten were to be sent to the seminary to become
teachers or rabbis. Hebrew was emphasized through the study
of all parts of the Bible. Biblical history was studied. The
curriculum included German, of course, both reading and
writing. Other subjects taught were French, history, geog-
raphy, drawing, singing, natural history, religion, morals,
"spiritual exercises," and practical ethics. Heroic efforts were
made to establish and reorganize elementary schools throughout the kingdom. A knowledge of Hebrew was emphasized
in all these schools that the children might understand the
prayers they recited. But great difficulties were met on all
sides due to the opposition of the people themselves. A universal difficulty in all these educational institutions was the
lack of proper textbooks. Some books already written by the
post-Mendelssohnians were used, and new ones, catechisms
for the youth and an epitome of the Mishneh Torah and an
introduction to the Talmud, were ordered written.[57]

Emancipation or adjustment, as Jacobson conceived it, was
to be both internal and external.[58] The Jew needed a religion
that, in its formal expression, in its ceremonial appearance,
would compare well with Christianity and convince the
Christian states that they had made no mistake in granting
Jews civil rights. It had to be, furthermore, a religion that
would ennoble and refine the Jews.[59] The inner Jewish religion had deteriorated because of the ceremonial husks that
surrounded it and threatened to choke it. The effort had to

be made to remove these husks and bring forth the original religion in its ancient purity. Through such a religion, the new generation, filled with modern ideas, could be held to Judaism. The task of purifying Judaism was one of the functions of the consistory as Jacobson conceived it. Jacobson determined to make changes because he felt that they were necessary.

He represented the point of view of a not inconsiderable group in Germany in the first two decades of the nineteenth century. This group had no sympathy for the radicals who scoffed at all religious ceremonies or for the Orthodox who steadfastly refused to adjust Judaism to what was certainly a new era. This was a group of laymen struggling to modernize Judaism against the protests of the mediaeval Orthodox rabbis who were completely at a loss in the new age and apparently unconscious of the problems of transition before them.[60] Nor was Jacobson in sympathy with the Friedlaender group which thought of establishing a cold natural religion based on the principles of eighteenth-century rational philosophy. Jacobson, rooted firmly in Orthodoxy, was too touched with pietism to countenance such a Judaism. His position in the parliament of Jewish thought is clear. At the extreme Right stood the last of the Orthodox rabbis, who were in a few years to denounce all changes. The Center included men like Berlin and Steinhardt, who rallied around Jacobson, men who were not unaware of the problems of the nineteenth century. Then came the Left, Jacobson. At the extreme Left stood Friedlaender, Benzeeb, and their friends.

The men of the Jacobsonian Left wanted to be Jewish in the traditional sense and also to be fully modern. They were dominated by the cultural ideals of the time. They wanted beauty and dignity in a religious service. Their rationalism had taught them to scoff at the mystical prayers of the cabalists. They wanted a refined occidental decorum. Their emotions were left untouched by prayers rattled off amidst noise and confusion. Their recently acquired sense of refinement was wounded by the lack of a devotional attitude. They wanted to remove abuses. There was as yet little desire to change the contents of the basic prayers. Theological differences were already felt by Jacobson, but his conservative environment in Westphalia and his own Orthodox emotional leanings forbade him to put them into practice. In theory Jacobson was theologically very liberal. This is clear from the Confession of Faith that he sent to the Minister of the Interior, von Wolffradt. The basis of Judaism, he said, was the Old Testament. Like all other religions, Judaism had three parts; it contained essential truths, customs, and relations with the state. These distinctions had to be made if the enlightened man did not wish to confuse the important with the unimportant. Essential truths were inviolable. They included the existence, the unity, and the perfection of God. God created everything into one harmonious whole. There was no reason to speculate on the pre-creation period. This would lead to doubt and indifference and was forbidden the Jew. Judaism was ready to define God negatively by asserting what He was not rather than by attempting to ascribe positive attributes to Him, for men could know nothing of Him. God had a purpose in creating man, for, as the highest intellect, He would do nothing irrational. God's purpose was a moral one, for He was good and holy and just and had moral desires.

These were the fundamental ideas of Jewish worship. To maintain these ideas, a Jew was obligated even to sacrifice his life and completely disregard all false prophets. The truth of these concepts was proved by creation, the Patriarchs, and the miraculous exodus. The above principles were spiritual and thus hard to understand by man who was only half spiritual. Man had to be taught by customs that appealed to the senses. The purer the religion, the more expedient in this respect were the customs. The Jew believed that custom as a part of revelation was also divine. Of course changes could be made if the Bible allowed it or life was in danger. The Bible taught, however, that the preservation of virtue was important, that the moral way of living was the right way of God. God looked more to morality than to observance of customs. The last thought Jacobson proved by an appeal to the Pentateuch and not to the prophets, where the proofs were more direct.

The third series of laws in a religion were those which determined its relation to the state. Jews were forbidden by the Bible—he quoted Deut. 17:8, 11, strangely enough, as proof—to form a state within a state. In all disputes of matters religious, the state had to decide. En passant, he emphasized that all the laws of the Hebrew Bible were not eternally binding, for it contained laws which applied only to certain individuals and were limited by time and locale. He finished his Confession by assuming that there were three degrees of devotion to Judaism. One might recognize all laws: moral and ceremonial and political. This would be possible only in the Orient, the land of origin of these laws. A second degree of devotion to the faith was a type of Orthodoxy where the customs were observed almost as much as the moral ideas. Here belief and customs were both essential. The highest degree of devotion was a more spiritual one. This type looked more to morals than to forms. It looked to the essential truths of religion without slavishly holding to individual customs, although customs were not to be despised or held lightly.

It is evident that Jacobson favored the more spiritual interpretation of Judaism. In this privately written Confession of Faith he showed his real attitude. It was essentially the faith of a man who considered binding upon himself only the spiritual values of the Old Testament. It was substantially the view of many Reformers in Germany in the first half of the nineteenth century. Jacobson often hinted at this attitude of his. It was surely known to his associates and his opponents, but he was never able to put it into practice. I am not even sure that, had the opportunity presented itself, he would have gone as far in actual practice as his written word required.[61] In the light of this Confession there can be no question that Jacobson was *in theory* a convinced Reform Jew.

Jacobson knew that there was a cultural chasm between him and the old-fashioned Jew. He was a nineteenth-century German in his appreciation of secular learning, in his exuberant loyalty to the state of which he was a citizen. But even in theology and religion the differences were vital, although Jacobson did not realize that he had really broken with the past. He honestly wanted to stand on Orthodox talmudic ground, yet he was constantly undermining himself. He observed all the holy days and the dietary laws and the major ritual commands. Yet he was striking at the root of Orthodoxy by the paring off of ceremonies and customs, thus impugning the important principle of the equal validity of all Jewish traditions. He made changes in many phases of life and custom, and one has the impression that the halachic justification was only an afterthought. He stressed the distinction between Jewish particularism and general universalism. He emphasized ethical and theological ideas over against ceremonial institutions. Ceremonialism was for him always subordinate and, in some instances, outworn. He was inclined to consider the Bible as the chief source of inspiration for Jewish life, and later development as a retrogression.

Jacobson and his friends scrupulously avoided rabbinic quotations in their sermons. After all, the Bible was the best book to show the common purposes of Judaism and Christianity. Jacobson was preparing the way for some later theological Reformers who emphasized the spiritual value of the biblical writings over against rabbinic literature. He thought that he was an Orthodox puritan. He thought that his reformation implied a clearing away of the accumulated accretions of the centuries, not a creation of the new. But he was wrong. He was really preparing the way for a complete religious reformation. Whether he wanted it or not, he was a theological reformer basing his changes on rational, philosophical grounds. The men who, after 1828, after his death, carried on his reforms were conscious of the dogmatic break with the past. They differed from Jacobson, however, not only in this realization, but also in the fact that they threw his rationalism overboard and proved his very contentions on historico-critical grounds.[62]

Possibly the most interesting phase of the religious development of the early nineteenth century in Germany was the almost complete collapse of rabbinic leadership. Laymen took over the leadership in that generation of transition, and it was not until about 1830 that the rabbis again recovered the reins of power both in liberal and in Orthodox circles. These laymen who tried to effect the religious transition were the teachers in the Jewish schools.[63] Out of these schools in the first twenty years of the century came the new service and the new ideas. Jacobson's religious activities at Seesen and Cassel were but one phase of this attempt on the part of lay teachers to bring about a Jewish renascence.[64] As early as 1802 the Jacobson school at Seesen conducted religious services for the children and the local Jews. The decorum was excellent.[65] In the consistorial school at Cassel in 1809 religious services were established where Jacobson himself spoke in the vernacular and prayers in German were read. All praying was done quietly. No chanting whatever was permitted, not even for the Torah reading. A song in Hebrew or German ended the service. Occasionally the parents of the children would come in, too.[66] Very probably he hoped that these services would set an example to be followed by others.[67]

His endeavors to bring about a worthy service culminated in the building and the dedication of the Seesen Temple.[68] The building itself was touched by classicism in its architecture. There was just a hint of rococo to point to the preceding century. This was the age of "empire." Simplicity, a return to nature, to primitive beauty, was the keynote of all life. There was a bell tower and a clock too. The religious service and dedication, however, were florid, almost baroque. The first modern service in its full form was held here—a German sermon and German prayers: German, not because of patriotism, but so that the Jew himself might understand what he read. The choir and congregation singing in German displaced the cantor singing in Hebrew. The group prayed as a whole rather than as individuals. This regimentation of prayer brought decorum. Decorum was lacking in the old school where prayer was the duty of an individual which he performed and then left. The well-trained choir and organ brought a strong sense of unity and discipline into everything. The service was dominated by the efficient Jacobson himself, who wore Protestant clerical garb. Through the leader unity in worship was attained. It was the victory of modern occidental decorum over oriental emotions; of enlightened despotism over Jewish individualism. At the end, everyone joined in singing "How great is the Almighty's Goodness" by Gellert, the famous Protestant moralist and writer.[69]

There were no avowed theological changes here, although there was a breaking with Jewish prejudices as sacred to the average worshipper as the fundamentals of the faith itself. Jacobson was proud of the dedication. He looked upon it as a great epoch-making event in Judaism. He held this service to show the world at large that Jewish worship could be made presentable. But the changes he made were not merely to satisfy his critical non-Jewish friends, but also to please the new Jewish generation which was estranged by the disorder of the old synagogue.[70]

It was an elaborate affair. Many Christian officials and clergymen came. Frenchmen and Germans, Jews, Catholics and Protestants were present. They were the guests of Jacobson at Seesen. There were banquets and processions. A choir of sixty to seventy voices, led by a Christian, fed the enthusiasm. Jew and Christian joined in the congregational singing. It was probably the first service where Jew and non-Jew sang together. A Christian who was there was impressed by the humanitarian and tolerant attitude of all those present. One of the Cathedral preachers of Halberstadt wrote a poem "The Christian in Jacob's Temple," and sang in his verses of Aaron's sons joining hand in hand with the faithful of the Roman and the Augsburg Confessions.

Jacobson's sermon on that memorable occasion has been preserved for us. As he built the temple, he bore in mind constantly the spirit of the time and the needs of his fellow-religionists. The problem of his fellow-Jews, he tells us, was the development of a proper religious education, a right observance of Jewish customs, and a true spiritual devotion. The prejudice which still existed between Jew and Christian had to be eliminated. This could be done best by beginning with the children, by encouraging the association of Jew and Christian. Jacobson did not want unity in religion. This was impossible. Differences between Jews and Christians in religious matters were vital. He said plainly that he did not want a common religion. The purpose of his temple was to carry on a Jewish service. He did not want to betray Judaism through new opinions and ideas. He reiterated his loyalty to the faith of his fathers. Yet Jews and Christians needed to be brought closer together. The Jews had to work together with the Christians, for through them would come the Jewish enlightenment, the development of pure religiousness, and the political welfare of the Jew. These were strong words. I know of no more radical, no rasher statements in all Jacobson's writings than these. I do not think that he was ever again as far to the Left as at that moment of enthusiasm.

Jewish worship, he continued, suffered from much that was useless. In part, it had degenerated into a spiritless saying of prayers and formulae which killed all devotion. Jewish religious principles were limited to a sum of knowledge which had not been improved for thousands of years. On all sides, Enlightenment opened invitingly for mankind. Were the Jews alone to stand back? Enlightenment was needed to help them forward. Jew and Christian had to be brought closer to each other through common progress towards the better: the final goal of reason. There had to be a purer God conception, a belief in His holiness, perfection, and unity. But dogmas were not the final purpose of a religious service. The ennobling of the heart and the practice of humanitarianism —these things were important. Religious worship founded on these principles would wipe away all enmity between religious groups. Both Jew and Christian had to be tolerant of one another. This was the great goal of all mankind. Jacobson prayed that his temple would be like the Temple of Solomon where even a stranger might come and find God. He hoped that the liturgy to be established at Seesen would further reverence, a sense of duty, moral equality, and also brotherly love. He dwelt here and elsewhere on the sufferings out of which the Jew had emerged. He spoke of the fatherland which no longer treated the Jew as an alien. Now that the Jew was free, his future would be determined by him alone. The Jew suffered from some religious customs which were antirational and offended his Christian friends. However, the consistory would remedy this situation.

As he was about to end his address, he turned to the Christians present who differed from him only in name and in a few matters of religion. He appealed to them to receive the Jew socially and in business life because the principles of Judaism as he had defined them should make the religion and the people acceptable everywhere. Judaism's religion was pure morality; its morals were rational; its attitudes were humanitarian. His final paragraph was an apostrophe to God and to religion. They were all brothers, Jews and non-Jews, and some day, when the fog was lifted from their eyes, they would all meet on the same path.[71] The universalism and humanitarianism of the preceding century stand revealed in every paragraph of his sermon. He was completely dominated by the rationalism of the last generation. In his address, Jacobson's definite distinction between the ceremonial, the dogmatic, and the religious in life stamped him unquestionably as a theological reformer in principle and intent. Conditions in Westphalia, however, made it difficult for him to carry out his ideas.

Religious services in the consistorial school at Cassel and in the temple at Seesen were but one phase of Jacobson's attempt to adjust Jewry to its new life. He felt he could best work through the decrees of the consistory which attempted to assume control over every phase of Jewish life. The idea of a complete control of Jewry, as complete as that under the old autonomous organization, still lurked in his mind. As a Court Jew and the son-in-law of a Court Jew, he could never free himself of the unconscious concept that Jewry should be autonomous and dominated by a Jew in authority. It must be said that, if Jacobson wished to exercise this power, it was always with a sense of obligation to his people. His was the highest type of enlightened despotism—a sense of obligation purified by moral and religious ideals laid down by the philosophers of the preceding century.

Early in 1810, Fraenkel, in an inspired article in *Sulamith*, threw an interesting light on the cultural progress of the German Israelites in Westphalia. His attitude certainly reflected that of Jacobson also. He asked for patience. He was speaking here to the small but insistent minority of radicals who demanded a complete break with the past. Fraenkel and Jacobson and Heinemann, the lay members of the consistory, certainly wanted more radical departures, but could do nothing because of the conservative character of the rabbinical members of the consistory, the government's suspicion of all sectarianism, and the resistance of the Jewish masses. Jacobson and his friends realized that too radical action would be inexpedient. They were prepared to work slowly and gradually for their "Reformation." They conceived of their changes as a minimum. They honestly believed that they had been very considerate of the prejudices of the people. This article laid down a program for coming legislation and carried a warning with it. All bad practices were to be removed to permit the real religion to come to the fore. This meant that the ceremonial acts and the religious services would be made more dignified. The Jews were asked to use the rights accorded them to turn to trade. More liberal laws were being made to allow the use of more vegetables and all kinds of sugar for the Passover, for the sake of the poor and the soldiers.[72] The consistory was to control the giving of rabbinical degrees and the right to slaughter. Rabbinical degrees and rabbinical responsa should not be paid for. Fraenkel appealed to the people, upon whose sympathy all depended, to help this work. He hoped that the religion which had sunk would now rise; that it would be respected by all peoples; that the children would become useful citizens of society.[73] He urged that this work go on so that the government would continue to look with favor on the Jews.

The consistory busied itself throughout the year 1810 in regulating the customs of Jewish marriage. Marriage customs that were, in its opinion, not justified were abolished by decree. Only the rabbis or someone else who could deliver a proper address should officiate. The *halizah* laws [with respect to levirate marriage] were modified to permit a widow to marry freely if her husband's brothers were away at war. A series of instructions was issued regulating the marriage laws so as to insure system and uniformity. Jacobson and his friends believed that uniformity was imperative in Jewish life if it was to be improved and saved from the vagaries of every different rabbi and leader. This desire to effect uniformity in thinking through a minutely prescribed discipline was the goal of every enlightened administrator in Europe. Every detail of the marriage ceremony was prescribed by the authorities in a manner worthy of the best traditions of the eighteenth-century police state and the Napoleonic system. An address in the vernacular was imperative. All other ceremonies not specifically mentioned in the decree were prohibited. Gone were the breaking of the glass, the singing of the cantor, the leading of the bride around the groom, the improper passing around of a flask instead of the use of wine glasses, the throwing of wheat grains on the bridal couple, and a number of other age-hallowed customs.[74]

In September of the same year,[75] a decree for the improvement of the religious services in the synagogue was issued. The various prohibitions of this law were a drastic break with traditions and folk-customs of long standing, traditions very dear to the untutored, stubborn, emotional masses.

This decree purported to remove from synagogal life those customs which had crept in and were unimportant. Some of these useless practices were no longer understood, some brought disruption into congregational life. Some had been declared inadmissible by former religious authorities, and some were out of joint with the times. Decorum and reverence were to be preserved within the sacred walls at all cost so that attendance in the synagogue would not continue to decrease. The president was made responsible in each community for decency and quiet in the house of worship. The good old knocking on the doors and inviting to services were forbidden. Everyone was required to come to the house of God clean and properly clad. Children under four were not to be admitted. While reading the liturgy, one no longer needed to wait for a cue from the rabbi. Itinerant cantors were forbidden to officiate. No one, whether a native or a foreigner, was to preach without permission of the consistory. This last was probably an attack on maggidim. *Meshorerim* (choristers) were also prohibited. Prayers were not to be shouted. The rabbi was not to preach about details of the Law or of cabala and mystical lore, but was to confine himself to religious and moral instruction. No business announcements were to be made at the service, but business notices could be nailed to the synagogue door, as was done in the churches. On all Sabbaths and holy days, prayers for the reigning dynasty were to be recited in the vernacular.

Kaddish (the prayer for the dead) was to be said quietly and in unison by the mourners. They were not to leave their places. Certain prayers were no longer to be sung, and others were to be recited only under certain prescribed circumstances. A man would be called to the Torah by his family name and not by the father's name. Abbreviations were taboo, and people who had not yet taken a family name were not to be called to the Torah. The singing that had accompanied the calling of the groom to the Torah was forbidden. The bar mizvah portion was not to be read out of the Torah, nor was the *tokehah* (Reproof Section, Lev. 26:14 ff.; Deut. 28:15 ff.) to be read differently from the rest of the Pentateuch. All men, married or unmarried, were permitted to read the haftarah (prophetical portion). The *ab ha-rahamim* ("Father of Mercy") prayer was forbidden. The reason for this last prohibition is obvious. The reproaches against those who had butchered the Jews were, for Jacobson, completely out of place in the new century that was ushering in love and friendship for the Jew.

This decree prescribed when and what piyyutim were to be recited. Some of the most famous were eliminated. Of more than passing importance is the prohibition against reading any piyyutim on the Ninth of Ab, the anniversary of the fall of the Temple. Jacobson's intention here was, I believe, to break with the tradition that the fall of the Temple was a national calamity. Some of the cabalistic prayers recited on Rosh Hashanah ("New Year") were omitted. Processions with the Torah on the eve of Simhat Torah ("Rejoicing of the Law") were forbidden. *Malkut* ("flagellation") in the synagogue before Yom Kippur ("the Day of Atonement") was forbidden. There was to be no Haman-klopfen, noise-making on Purim. In the event these laws were not obeyed, the synagogues would be closed and the cantors removed. Like most canon law, the decrees could not easily be enforced, but it was all very indicative of the attitude of Jacobson and his group. We may safely assume that he would have gone further, had not his rabbinical associates checked him. The principles that motivated the changes made in this decree were not new. They had been preached by liberals and radicals for a generation, and the organization Felix Libertate of Amsterdam had, about fifteen years earlier, fought for reform in the synagogal service. It had demanded the removal of the piyyutim and the changing of those prayers which emphasized social opposition or political differences between Jew and Gentile.[76] Jacobson was fully aware of these Jewish currents in Holland.

A royal order was promulgated in 1811 forbidding private religious services.[77] Penalties were to be imposed for all those who violated this law by attempting to gather for worship outside of the community synagogue. Jacobson's purpose here was to introduce his own standardized service throughout the country, and he resented the efforts of the Orthodox to frustrate his desires. Because he felt that he was doing right, he felt no compunctions about limiting freedom of worship. When, in a few years, he went to Berlin and established a Reform service, he insisted there that private religious services be permitted him, for he was then in opposition to the standardized Orthodox service of the community. Even as he had stopped dissenting services in Westphalia, so in Berlin his dissenting synagogue was closed, and it almost broke his heart. The tolerance which he refused to accord, he demanded of others. Like all men passionately engrossed in a great idea, he was blind to the other man's point of view. I suspect that Jacobson, although a very witty and genial man, completely lacked a sense of humor.

Jacobson felt that he was successful in Westphalia. He was not unconscious of the powerful opposition that he had to cope with on all sides. He could not have hidden from it had he wanted to do so. He knew all the time what he would have to meet. Yet he looked upon his work as a success. He gloried in the fact that, during his stay, the Jews had become full-fledged citizens; that schools for religious and moral instruction had been built; that the service had been refined; that a better system and order had been established in Westphalian Jewry and, as he felt, were on their way to observance.[78]

Jacobson's work did not meet with a hearty response on the part of the Jews in the conglomerate known as Westphalia. The individuality of the several states that made up this kingdom impressed itself on their respective Jewries. Each group had its own rights and religious traditions and did not care to surrender them at the command of Jacobson and the consistory. Jacobson himself was bound by the conservative character of his rabbinical associates on the Consistorial Board. They zealously watched that no action be taken which would mark any violent departure from rabbinical Judaism.[79] On Shabuot (Pentecost), 1811, Schott at Seesen held a confirmation service. Part of the ritual employed by the children was written by a Pastor Goecking, of Roessing. The consistory rebuked

Schott for this vigorously despite the fact that he was an intimate associate of Jacobson.

Jerome Bonaparte, the king, was not in sympathy with all
the changes sponsored by Jacobson.[80] The people as a whole
were opposed to almost every change that was made. They
seemed to be in opposition to everything that implied changes
or taxes. They were opposed to the consistory itself, even
though it marked an obvious change for the better. Despite
the fact that the taxes imposed by the consistory were far less
than those in the pre-French days, they protested and howled
lustily.[81] Still, times were hard, for the profligacy of Jerome
and the constant state of war were weighing heavily on
the whole land. This constant interplay of retarding and
oppositional forces made progress difficult. In its attempt to
placate all groups, the consistory moved in some ceremonial
matters with exceeding caution, yet on occasion it plunged
ahead in a manner that evinced neither deliberation nor in-
telligence.[82] But nothing that the consistory did pleased the
people, particularly when they realized—as they soon did—
that most consistorial decress had no teeth.[83]

They objected to every modification, no matter how small,
in their ceremonial and religious life. They denied the right of
the consistory to make religious changes. They even attacked
Jacobson before the king. The statements of the consistory
were usually of an apologetic nature, appealing for support,
although the resort to threats was not uncommon. In 1812,
Mendel Steinhardt wrote his *Dibre Iggeret,* an attempt to
justify the ritual changes and to show that many were based
on the best Jewish authorities.[84] He insisted that the purpose
of the consistory was to teach a proper Judaism, and he inveighed against those ignoramuses who held fast to every
minhag.[85] He justified certain liturgical alterations on the

basis of decorum and true religious sentiment. Anti-Gentile phrases, he pointed out, had been removed because they might have involved Jews in trouble, and Jews were, after all, well treated now.[86] Some Jewish leaders took the oath to support the consistory, but qualified it by saying that they would not consider themselves bound to accept changes already made or to be made.[87] Some were angry because the attempt to control the officiants at Jewish ceremonies—preachers, ritual slaughterers, and teachers—struck at their economic life or that of their friends.

In his home town, Halberstadt, Jacobson experienced bitter opposition. His youthful friends believed that he was influenced for the worst by the Cassel environment and particularly by Schott, a "devotee of the superficial rationalism and the destructive tendencies of the Berlin reformers." It was, they believed, Schott who had moved him to make these inroads "into historic Judaism and the freedom of the conscience of the individual." Orthodoxy has a touching and dramatic story, probably true, too, how the great Akiba Eger was commanded by the absolutistic consistory to close the Klaus Synagogue, and as he was mournfully surrendering the key to the police, the good news came that the consistory had been abolished. Some of the Jews of Halberstadt refused to attend Shabuot services in the community synagogue because a number of piyyutim had been removed. So Aron Hirsch and others held a private service which was well attended, and after it was through, they walked over to the mayor's office, admitted their guilt, and paid the 1,000-franc fine.[88]

From an Amsterdam rabbi came a protest against German prayers in the synagogue.[89] Jacobson was hurt at the opposition to the German prayers and wrote the rabbi of Brunswick, Sabel Eger, to ask the reason why. Eger pointed out to him that the furthering of German in the liturgy—disregard for Hebrew—would mean the gradual disappearance of an educated Jewish laity and the breaking of the strongest bonds that united Jewry everywhere.[90] The people and their rabbis, with few exceptions, resented the Passover dispensations. They felt that these things should have been left to the individual conscience. Eger admitted the value of some of the reforms in the service for those Jews who were almost out of the fold. This might bring them back. Yet he warned Jacobson that the proposed changes would cause a lot of trouble. Fraenkel's statement that certain prayers had to be eliminated—even though they came from the Men of the Great Synagogue itself—because they were out of joint with the times, encouraged fanaticism, and hindered purity of feeling brought forth a strong objection from Eger. He resented any move that touched the authority of the *Shulchan Aruk*. Eger realized the important principle involved in the attack on the binding character of the ceremonial law. His objection to the Passover dispensations was characteristic. He looked upon the request made by the consistory that the rabbis lead in eating the permitted Passover foods as a violation of conscience.

Even the Central Consistory of French Jewry in Paris was astonished at the Passover dispensations and asserted that Jacobson's consistory had not sufficient authority for such legislation. The French wrote Jacobson that many people had protested to them. They were surprised that such action had been taken without asking other religious officials for advice.[91] The French Consistory did not interfere in matters of belief or practice. It was merely a passive administrative unit limiting itself to the functions specifically assigned it. Jacobson had ideas and a philosophy of life and was not content to approve mechanically the orders of the government above him or to reflect the wishes of the masses beneath him.

Was the opposition of the masses and their rabbis in West-phalia justified? To a large extent, it was. But it was a difficult situation. A Jewry that had been cast in a certain mold since the fourth Christian century was face to face with a new world. Changes were imperative. Jacobson realized this, but most rabbinic leaders did not. Jacobson determined to effect the necessary transition in Westphalia himself. His method of procedure was rooted completely in an enlightened despotism and a rationalistic, moralistic, pedantic religious philosophy. He tried to force a transition hurriedly. A true child of his time, he had no knowledge or appreciation of the necessity of gradual historic change. In his *Humble Remonstrance* to the Prince-Primate of Frankfort, he had declared that Judaism would satisfy the demands of the state, if the state did not interfere. A state could not refine a religion. A religion had to ennoble and refine itself. Beautiful words, but he had forgotten all about them that same year as he set about arbitrarily re-forming Jewry in Westphalia. He and his friends felt Jewry was debased—albeit due to Christian intolerance—and they were determined to "further culture and humanity among the Jewish nation." [92]

His consistorial group had the outlines of a program but could not agree on its details. They rallied around Jacobson, but it is difficult to determine if they knew where they were going. Jacobson was hardly the man for the task to which he had set himself. There was not one Jew on the consistory who had a good, sound academic training. Jacobson himself did not have the general or Jewish scholarly training for the task which he had undertaken.[93]

The success he craved could not be assured by mere administrative ability. He was magnificently energetic and sincere in all that he did, but he did not have the vision for his task. He did not estimate its difficulties, and he did not realize his own limitations. He believed that hard work and good will and authority would solve all problems. He was not a radical, but his liberalism was far too extreme for the mass of people whom he asked to follow him. He was very arbitrary. The old Court Jews and the Christian princelings were tyrannical, but even they had never attempted to prescribe the details of Jewish ritual and observance. Jacobson did. He did violence to the conscience of every Jew by his decrees.

He was a curious contradiction. He was a thoroughgoing individualist in his protest against the established order in Jewish things, yet he employed the most conservative, authoritarian method of effecting his liberal reforms. The paradox is only apparent. It was the ambition of this man, who was not a radical by nature, to fit his people into an already established cultural mold. To Jews of his day, he appeared a radical, but to the Protestant Church of his time and to himself, the Jew with a secular background, his action of attempted adjustment was merely an acceptance of the normal established culture. Hence he was no real liberal from the point of view of his cultured non-Jewish contemporaries. He never ventured outside the range of ideas of the average enlightened Protestant churchman. His acts were liberal only when viewed from the vantage point of Orthodox Jewry.

He never realized that his people, whom he really loved, knew nothing about philosophic criticisms of ceremonialism and that they cared even less. He was a man with a great deal of influence, but he did not use it intelligently. In one of his humble moments, in his letter to von Wolffradt, he spoke of himself as a businessman, not a learned man. Yet he attempted the solution of problems that only scholars and recognized authorities should have attempted. He sought to reform Judaism and to fit it into a new world. The rabbis should have done all this, but they were hopelessly unprepared for the work. Jewry faced a crisis, but its rabbis and its scholars were helpless. They did not even realize the problem. So Jacobson, the layman, unfit, was chosen for the task and bungled it. It was unfortunate, historically, that two laymen, Abraham Furtado in France and Jacobson in Westphalia, had so much influence. Since they were not rooted in a profound knowledge of Jewish life, their solution was one of expediency. They were desirous of making peace with the state at almost any price. They had no appreciation of the continuity of Jewish life as reflected in its ceremonial and ritual. The masses, however unthinkingly, had a finer appreciation of Jewish values. They resented bitterly the changes in Westphalia and refused to accept them. Like Joseph II and other enlightened despots, Jacobson tried to emancipate from above, by decree, without thought of the receptivity of the people.

Jacobson, as a layman, a man of affairs, thought primarily of an external adjustment. Enlightenment was for him almost synonymous with harmonization with the dominant Christian culture. He wanted Jewry to look like the Christian groups about him. He introduced Christian customs, ceremonies, and dress into Judaism. This was tactless. His people had known only the ruder side of their Christian associates and resented this hasty and forced rapprochement. The Germanic elements he introduced into his ritual were not basically Jewish, but were reflections of the general philosophic and moral teachings of his day. He abolished whatever he thought retarded the progress of his people without reflecting that he was cutting away customs so ingrown in Jewish life that they could not be removed without affecting the religion itself. Jacobson was dominated by current philosophic ideas, not Jewish thinking.

His writings and preachings were not distinctively Jewish. They were filled with the spirit of a wide universalism, beautiful in itself, fine, possibly, as a program for future generations, but woefully inadequate for the slowly-emerging, stubbornly-resisting granite masses of his own day. The change Jacobson desired could be established only through a sound, critical, and constructive knowledge of Judaism on the part of the leaders and the masses. This knowledge was woefully absent in all. It took another generation, led by Zunz, to build a scientific and sounder background for Jewish life in the nineteenth century.[94]

It is true the masses were opposed to the consistory; it is true Jacobson and his group made serious errors in their conduct of Jewish affairs, yet even these circumstances could not have stopped their work. The opposition of the people was active but unorganized. The charm, the ceaseless activity, and unfailing generosity of Jacobson went far to cover up his mistakes in judgment. Had he been allowed to carry on undisturbed by political events, he and Jewry might ultimately have fumbled through to a Jewish life that would have been both modern and thoroughly Jewish. But the Napoleonic system was nearing its collapse. On September 28, 1813, the Cossacks of Chernyshëv were at the doors of Cassel. Jacobson realized what this meant to his plans. He held a service for succor, in the synagogue, but all in vain. A month later, Napoleon had been defeated at Leipzig, the following month Jerome left Cassel, and, in December, Jacobson himself moved on.[95] The consistory was dead, and with it fell its decrees and reforms. He knew that this was the end of his dreams. What brought victory to the Germans brought destruction to him. The allied victory meant the fall of French Westphalia and her program of equality for all citizens.[96] It is ironically symbolic that the Central European political reaction which now began was, one might say, ushered in by Russian Cossacks. It was this same political reaction that made a free, unfettered development of Reform Judaism impossible in Germany.[97]

As Jacobson left the consistory in the winter of 1813, he may have believed that all his work was in vain. It looked that way. Today we realize that his Westphalian adventure was epoch-making in Judaism. He tried to do away with the debris of centuries. He worked hard to mold a religious service that would be beautiful and acceptable. He introduced decorum and a sense of reverence into worship. Music in the form of choral singing and instrumental accompaniment was ushered in. The use of the vernacular in the liturgy and in preaching was brought back to Jewish life. The rounded-out aesthetic service that he developed pleased some Jews who had found no comfort or true religion in the worship of their co-religionists. These men he kept in the fold.[98] He thus did effective work in stopping conversion and indifference. He emphasized the need for a sound, general education for all Jews, both men and women, young and old. He realized fully the character of the modern state and understood that mediaeval Jewish autonomy was a thing of the past. He knew that the Jew would have to live more intimately with his political and social environment. He attempted to further this rapprochement. He wanted to make the Jew an integral part of the new state. He tried to point out how a man might remain a true Jew and yet be a truly modern citizen. During his six-year stay in Westphalia, he helped to further Jews as teachers, jurists, civil service officials, and soldiers.[99]

The generation since the death of Mendelssohn had been characterized by an effort toward self-emancipation. There was a strong movement to leave the exclusive rigidity of the past and to enter boldly and willingly into the new life of the present. Jacobson was one of those who succeeded in entering into the modern world without denying or breaking off all attachments to the past. He was a pioneer.[100] He still remained within the fold of a nominal Orthodoxy, but he prepared the way for the Reform Jewish theology of the nineteenth century. He pointed the way by the distinction that he accepted between essentials and nonessentials in Jewish thinking and living; by his acknowledgement of the right of an age to make necessary changes; by his reluctance to retain the purely politico-nationalistic ideas in Judaism.[101] Through his organ, *Sulamith,* the first German Jewish periodical, his ideas had gone all over Europe.[102]

The Israel Jacobson whom we knew as a Jewish emancipator, educator, and religious reformer had during these Westphalian days another side to his being. He played an important part in the public life of the state apart from his Jewish work. It was the influence that he developed in this sphere that stood him in good stead in his efforts on behalf of his people.

He kept open house at Woeltingerode where Christian scholars and theologians would visit him. He is reported to have been a very congenial host.[103] He was a representative in the legislature[104] and busied himself with raising money for the needy state. He went to Holland for this purpose, but did not succeed, even though he was willing to share part of the loan himself. Jerome, the spendthrift, was heavily in debt to Jacobson. By the middle of 1809, the king owed him about a million and a half francs. Jacobson carried on huge financial operations with the government throughout this period. The French were secularizing the large church estates, and Jacobson bought a number of cloisters, including even pictures of the saints. Woeltingerode, his home, was one of these old cloistral properties.[105]

Jacobson, we see, was one of the leading financiers of the king and the government, and the influence he thus secured aided him in his position as president of the consistory. His unquestioned generosity and honesty did not prevent him from attempting to pay as little income tax as possible. This appears to be quite a human trait.[106] It is by no means improbable that the complaints that he did not pay sufficient taxes were inspired by the old Brunswick official clique that was still in power and still went out of its way to annoy him.

He was greatly respected. Napoleon's minister in Cassel wrote back to France very highly of him, and B. C. W. Spieker, a Christian, dedicated his work on the Jews to Jacobson.[107] His activity on behalf of the state brought him honors. He was made court banker and a knight of the Order of the Crown of Westphalia.[108] His personal life inspired the respect if not the affection of the people. He entertained King Jerome when the school at Seesen was inspected.[109]

Despite his display of energy Jacobson was not a healthy man. In 1810, he went to the Helmstedt baths and, after a successful stay, established an endowment to provide for baths for the sick poor. He also built a bridge over a swampy part of the road.[110] In the summer of 1813, he visited the health resort of Nenndorf, officiated in the local synagogue as Chazzan, and also preached several times. He showed himself there very genial and friendly to rich and poor alike. He observed the dietary laws.[111]

Throughout this Westphalian period, in spite of his great wealth, he lived modestly. There was no luxury in his home. He believed in hard work. He boasted to his friends, as he preached at the marriage of his daughter, that he had earned his money through hard work and had oppressed no man. In this interesting sermon, he inveighed against luxury, telling his children to help the poor, and he also informed us, rather naively, that he still loved his wife as much now, many years after their marriage, as on the first day of their union. He wanted his daughter to live in such a way that people would say: "These parents have reared good children; they have given the state useful citizens."[112]

5.   Berlin

After the collapse of the Westphalian Kingdom, Jacobson went for a time to his estate at Woeltingerode and finally, in 1814, to Berlin. He could not remain in Cassel under her restored rulers, and he would not return to Brunswick. He knew that there his business enemies would, under the guise of patriotism, make his life miserable.[1]

Many reasons impelled him to go to Berlin. The Prussian kingdom, in its decade of humiliation at the hands of the French, had realized that it needed inner consolidation. Only a united and transformed Prussia could hope to maintain herself. Out of this period of inward searching came the decree of March 11, 1812, emancipating Prussian Jewry. Jacobson, therefore, was happy to go to Berlin, for he wished to be associated with a politically emancipated Jewry. Berlin was one of the few cities in Germany where he could hope to find a group sympathetic to his ideas. Hardenberg, his friend, was chancellor. Berlin was an inviting field of activity for him. Jacobson did not intend to stop his work because his Westphalian venture had come to a violent end. He knew there were great opportunities for him in Berlin, and he was determined to take advantage of them.

Religious and cultural conditions in Berlin were chaotic. The old rabbis were no longer regarded. The fateful year of 1812 had opened to Prussian Jewry the vista of more intimate contacts with Gentile fellow-citizens. Some Jews, intoxicated with this thought, had thrown their faith overboard. Many adopted a superficial, cynical attitude toward all things religious, a complete indifference to the ancestral creed. The synagogues were empty. A change in the inner life of Jewry was an absolute necessity; some form of adjustment to the new cultural world was imperative.

107

Friedlaender, in 1812 and 1813, attacked the problem from the religious side. He proposed to reform Jewry in order to modernize it. He wanted to change radically the forms and content of Jewish worship. He was a German nationalist and patriot. Prussia was his fatherland; German his national tongue. He was openly opposed to Jewish national prayers and the messianic hopes of the liturgy. He wanted a German prayer book. But he accomplished nothing. His wish to reduce Judaism to a simple system of morals and to eliminate the specific Jewish character of the synagogue did not appeal even to his own friends. His radical religious deism was totally foreign to Jewish life. Hardenberg approved his ideas, but the king, a timid conservative, feared his new teachings and objected decidedly. One Jewish leader attacked Friedlaender, but admitted the need for improvement; another appealed to the chancellor for a reorganization of Prussian Jewry along Jacobsonian lines.[2]

Then Jacobson came. People expected a great deal of him. He was a recognized and distinguished figure. He soon gathered a following about him, for they knew he was an experienced religious reformer. There were people in Berlin who sincerely desired to solve their problems. Jacobson won them over. He was wealthy and generous, he was friendly and sincere. He was enthusiastic. He was known as a liberal, but not as a radical. He seemed to be an ideal leader.[3]

His position in Berlin, however, was far different from what it had been in Westphalia. There he had been the first Jew in the kingdom; emancipator, educator, and religious reformer. Here he was an outsider. He was not even a citizen. The community as a whole was Orthodox. He could not hope to dominate it either through his personality or any office that he might be granted in it.

Yet he was determined, like Friedlaender before him, to begin his work by reforms in the religious life. Jacobson concentrated on matters religious because this was the only field of endeavor really open to him now. In Berlin, therefore, he was primarily a religious reformer. He probably thought that a new type of service would stem the tide of religious indifference among the enlightened and help Orthodoxy by giving it a more intelligent and spiritual appreciation of Judaism. This did not mean that he had given up his interest in Jewish education and emancipation. Not at all. Jacobson was interested in the Association of Friends which first furthered education for Jewish children in Berlin and Germany. In 1815, just after he came to the Prussian capital, he was made a member of one of the most important committees of this organization. When he died, he left it a legacy of 300 talers.[4]

He did not feel called upon now to play the part of an emancipator. He did not feel that there was any further need for intercession here after the passing of the decree of March, 1812. When an occasion arose on which his people did need him, he did not fail to respond. The year after he came to Berlin, a satire on Jewish life called *Die Judenschule* was about to appear. A number of friends at Jacobson's home told him of its anti-Jewish character. He immediately rushed over to Hardenberg and had it forbidden. He was determined to protect his people at all cost. Two months later, the same comedy appeared under a different name. Jacobson's rash intervention had only served to make it a sure success.[5]

Shabuot, 1815, Jacobson held his first Reform service in Berlin. The occasion was the confirmation of his son Naphtali. It was a private home service. Christians and Jews were present. From that day on, every Saturday morning, from eight till ten, religious services were held in his home. The room was lit up with candles, even though it was broad daylight. Jacobson led in prayer, pronouncing the Hebrew after the Sephardic manner. He had learned this probably in Amsterdam. Men and women sat separately. The hat, of course, was worn. There was a choir in which children sang; an organ furnished the accompaniment. Christians, too, were employed in the choir.[6] The most important prayers were still recited in Hebrew, although there were German prayers too. German songs were sung all through the service. Jacobson handed out cards informing the people that they were to read the Torah, for there was no public summons. The Torah, too, was read with the Sephardic pronunciation; there was no Ashkenazic intoning. Before the reading of the weekly portion from the Bible, Jacobson himself would preach. Occasionally he would invite some of the young men about him to give the sermon. The sermon at once became a very important part of the service. The Eighteen Benedictions were not repeated; the entire Additional, or musaf, prayer was omitted. Considerations of brevity, no doubt, underlay these changes. No definite theological motives seem to have found expression in this service, which, planned in the interests of expediency, was short, attractive, and not offensive to the Gentiles. Even some of the radicals were in sympathy with Jacobson. Friedlaender and Bendavid gave their moral support; all actual expenses were borne by Jacobson himself.[7]

The success of this new form of worship was immediate. There was a not inconsiderable group in the city to whom Jacobson appealed. He knew what they wanted. They wanted a service that was aesthetically proper. They wanted refinement and decorum, devotion and reverence in worship. All this was lacking in the communal Orthodox service. They wanted good, modern music. They wanted the Hebrew prayers pronounced intelligibly. Jacobson approved of their wishes and satisfied them. He believed, too, that a beautiful worship service would stimulate sympathy for religion itself. The Westphalian influence is obvious here, for this service was very much like the one that he had introduced there. Large crowds came, and soon the quarters in Jacobson's home were too small. Jacob Herz Beer, the father of Meyerbeer, the composer, opened a hall in his house where the people met from then on.[8]

But the services so auspiciously begun soon came to an inglorious end. They lasted only about eight months. That same year, December 9, 1815, the king intervened and forbade the service. Herz Beer protested in vain. The next month, on January 28, 1816, the king confirmed his previous action and gave his reasons in detail. The synagogue, not a private home, was the proper place for worship. If the majority did not understand the Hebrew prayers, then it was their obligation to induce the rabbis, the proper authorities, to make changes or translations. Under no circumstance was sectarianism to be permitted.[9] There can hardly be any doubt that the action of the king was inspired by the protests of the Orthodox wing. But Jacobson and his friends were not idle. They were not without a powerful following. As a matter of fact, the leaders of the Jewish community were in sympathy with them and had attended their services. Unfortunately for them, the unenlightened rank and file were Orthodox.

Through the connivance of their friends in the Community Directorate and no doubt through influence with the liberal Hardenberg, the Jacobson-Beer temple was reopened on New Year (Rosh Hashanah), 1817. It was now tolerated by the authorities because it was to serve as an interim-synagogue until the small community had been rebuilt. Jacobson was the dominant spirit in this new venture, and, of course, he and Herz Beer continued the Reform service they had already inaugurated.[10]

In order that the services might be properly carried on, two song books and two prayer books were published. The official prayer book was called *Prayers for Sabbath Morning And the Two Days of New Year*. Kley and Guensburg, protégés of Jacobson, published a prayer book, privately, in 1817. This was called *The German Synagogue . . . for Communities That Use German Prayers.*

The changes in the prayer book sponsored by Jacobson and his friends were not essential. More German was used than in 1815, but the Additional (musaf) prayer was reintroduced. Jost, the historian, believed that in the Berlin service, beginning with 1815, Jacobson paid more attention to traditional prejudices than in Westphalia, for he realized he had gone too far. These services were more Jewish. Jost, we know, was conversant with both services, the Westphalian and the Berlin. Yet I question if Jacobson was more conservative because he realized he had plunged too far ahead. If he made concessions, I believe it was because he wished to attract the Orthodox and to induce them to accept his ritual as the official, communal one. Jacobson in matters like this could be very opportunistic; Friedlaender was far more intransigent and consistent.[11]

The holy day prayers were the same as those recited by the Orthodox except that the piyyutim, the poetical insertions, were limited. There were in reality no changes here to which one might have objected on theological grounds. The prayer book of Kley and Guensburg was slightly different. The service was shortened considerably. It was of this tendency to limit the prayers that Jellinek made his famous pun: "And he said to the 'cutters,' The Lord be with you."[12] The few changes found here show the way the wind was blowing. Practically all references to Zion and sacrifice were retained, yet in one place the phrase "the days of the Messiah" was changed to "the days of redemption." The prayer "Restore . . . our land" was altered, and the musaf prayer was omitted. Some of the blessings recited with the prophetical portion (haftarah) were omitted because they referred to King David, yet others that referred to Zion were retained.

In both these prayer books, there is no consistency. They betray the uncertainty of Jacobson and his time. It was a generation in transition, a generation that turned its face to the future, but stood in the past. The theological disparity here between the old and the new was minimal, yet the acrimony between the two groups was intense. There was a sharp line of cleavage already made between the party that was determined to hold to the old and the party that was equally determined to assimilate itself to the new. The differences, slight as they were, were magnified and served as a battleground on which the quarrel was fought out.[13]

The Orthodox could not worship in the old synagogue now under repair, and they refused to listen to the new ritual in the Jacobson-Beer temple. They could not conscientiously tolerate prayers and sermons and songs in the vernacular, to say nothing of organ music and the omission of prayers. They produced the responsa of rabbis who condemned the Reform service, and they pointed to the new Hamburg Temple as an evidence of the confusion in Jewish life. The two parties could not agree or compromise, and the state finally intervened by appointing a commission to settle the matter. But the commission could not accomplish anything either. All sorts of compromises were proposed by the liberal party, but the Orthodox were adamant. They carried their objections to the king himself, and he listened to them. He had never been in sympathy with the revival of the Jacobson-Beer temple in 1817. He did not like "arbitrary novelties." He made his decision clear in a decree of the 9th of December, 1823. Jewish worship, he said, was to be held only in the local (communal) synagogue, only according to the traditional liturgy, without the slightest change in speech, ceremony, prayer, or song. It had to be in complete accord with ancient tradition. He would, he ended, tolerate no sect among the Jews of his states.[14]

The experiment had not lasted ten years. It was the king's action, more than anything else, that brought to an end in the Prussian state the reforming efforts of Jacobson and his friends. Hardenberg had died the year before. As long as he lived, the liberal group had a friend at court. The Ministers of State were themselves not unsympathetic, but Frederick William III, who had lived through the sad days of Napoleonic control, was suspicious of any form of liberalism. Gabriel Riesser believed that the king, through his prohibition of a modern service, aimed at driving the Jews into the bosom of the Christian Church, but I do not think that this motive prompted the decrees of Frederick William III.[15]

A great change had come into German life since 1815, the fall of Napoleon. The Holy Alliance between Russia, Austria, and Prussia, which was formed originally to further a patriarchal-Christian government, soon turned against all free ideas in political and intellectual life. Conservatism was the order of the day. In literature and in national sentiment, a Romanticism had arisen that looked to the German national past for inspiration rather than to humanity at large. A passionate love for everything Christian and German filled the hearts of many—a love that was so particularistic that it could not include the Jews. It was to meet this new German nationalism that Jacobson and his disciples thought it advisable to curtail the references to the restoration of a political Zion. The political and cultural conservatism of Gentile Prussia, the principle of historicity and legitimacy, no doubt, reacted on an impressionable Jewry and made it also averse to any changes. Reaction was in the air.

Jacobson showed no trace in his life of the German Romantic movement. It was spiritually impossible for him. He had always preached universal humanity and rapprochement. How could he adjust himself or his Judaism to an exclusive, separatistic German nationalism? How could he, rooted in the universal principles of liberalism, look with favor upon a mystical Romanticism that was anti-rational and anti-Jewish? As a humanitarian and a Jew it was unacceptable to him. The times were fighting against him. The tolerant Enlightenment was dead, but Jacobson did not know it; he did not dare realize it.

Beginning again with 1815, the Jew in Germany was attacked on the stage, in literature, and even on the streets. In 1817 there was a union of the Reformed and the Lutheran Church in Prussia. It is easy to understand why a king who wanted unity in Protestantism would not encourage sectarianism in Judaism. In 1818, the Jews were expelled from Luebeck; the following year, De Wette, professor of theology in Berlin, was deposed for his political liberalism. This same year, a German political reaction under the influence of Metternich set in sharply. In South Germany, the mob turned against the Jews and killed several. The privileges of the edict of 1812 were limited through interpretation. Missionary societies were encouraged. Christian children were forbidden to attend Jewish schools. This was the sorry background for a

Reform movement in Germany, and it is by no means surprising that it made so little progress.[16] The people were distracted from pursuing religious ideals. From the days of Mendelssohn to the fall of Napoleon, Jewry had been busy freeing itself culturally from the past and modernizing itself. The new problem, now that the political reaction had set in, was to free the Christian state from its prejudices against Jewry so that the political emancipation might be complete and wholehearted. This problem rather than the religious one absorbed the attention of many Jews.[17]

After the open opposition of the king, interest on the part of many Jews in Reform services began to decline. It is not at all improbable that Jewry itself began to be touched by the antirational and mystical spirit of the decade and turned away from the beautiful but anemic services.

There were many inherent faults in Jacobson's work, and it may be questioned if all his reforms would have maintained themselves, even if untoward circumstances had not destroyed his work. Most of the preachers who had helped him were not at home in Jewish lore. Their sermons were not particularly Jewish. One might well substitute the word Christian for Israelite and have a good Protestant sermon. Even the homilies of Zunz, the father of Jewish scholarship, were not particularly Jewish, although they already mirrored his interest in history and his love for his people. Yet the apologetic spirit was present in him, too. Out of a clear sky, he closed one of his sermons with the statement: The highest, my friends, you must dedicate to your fatherland, to this land, to which you belong.[18]

Jacobson and his friends were too busy convincing Gentiles that they were not unpatriotic and not barbarians. They went out of their way to please a few Christian liberals with their services at a time when mobs in Bavaria were attacking and killing Jews. Jacobson made little attempt to retain the specific confessional character of the Jewish service hallowed by centuries of folk-custom. He threw it all overboard because, according to the standard of the age, it was unrefined and out of joint with the times. Neither he nor any of the young preachers about him seem to have had any conscious program of principle beyond the one of setting up a beautiful service. They emphasized the form and completely neglected the content of Jewish teaching. The preachers had little real authority anyhow. The wealthy lay leaders were in complete control.[19] Jacobson evidently thought that, through the acceptance of his ritual, the Jew as Jew would solve all his problems in Prussia. He thought that the old Orthodox service had destroyed religion in the Jew, and his new service would restore it. He did not have the insight to understand the aversion of the Orthodox to his new ideas, and he did not realize that more than negative changes and a flaccid system of morals was necessary to bring educated Jewry back into the fold.[20]

As a matter of fact, a number of keener minds of the Reform wing realized that there was too much show, too little inner religiosity and understanding of Judaism, and actually welcomed the royal decree prohibiting everything.[21] Its very friends and preachers felt it was doomed: Jost, Mannheimer, and Zunz. Zunz, its preacher for a couple of years, felt its decay was caused not only by its followers, but also by its leaders. Heine was brilliantly vicious and discerning in his attacks. There was no real harmony on the board of administrators.[22]

It was not Jacobson's fault that he had no sound knowledge of the ideals of Judaism or of its history and development. There was no "Science of Judaism" in his day to enlighten the naive layman. It is one of the curious ironies of history that the same year that Zunz published his first great essay, Jacobson's health broke down, and he ceased to play an active part in the German Reform movement.[23] This year, 1818, was pointing out the way that Reform would have to take in order to live and thrive. But now, deprived of Jacobson's constant leadership and support, the Reform movement in Berlin declined until it was annihilated by the decree of Frederick William III.

A year before Jacobson became ill, in 1817, he exerted himself to help those Jews in the Free City of Hamburg who contemplated a Reform service. Their leader at first was Kley and later Gotthold Salomon. The latter had preached for Jacobson in Berlin. The former was one of his disciples who had gone in 1817 to Hamburg as a teacher when he realized that there was no future for his ideas in the Prussian lands.

That same year, through Kley, a "New Israelitish Temple Association, which appealed to Jacobson for aid. He wrote to wanted an acceptable aesthetic religious service.[24] This association did not intend to introduce theological novelties. Kley, certainly influenced by Jacobson's teachings, gave them a modern service. The Orthodox here now turned against the Association, which appealed to Jacobson for aid. He wrote to the influential Lazarus Riesser, of Luebeck, and besought him to look favorably on the Hamburg experiment. But he asked for more. He wished to know if it would be possible to induce all of Hamburg Jewry to unite under a modernized service.

Riesser answered his friend Jacobson that he was bound by his innermost being to the form as well as to the content of Judaism. In the last thirty years, he said, a large number of the followers of all the religions, including the Jewish, had thrown aside all form in religion and wished only to retain the essence. Because it was impossible to hold on to the essence without the form, untoward results had set in. The non-Jews had already discovered that they had gone too far, and even the Jews were already beginning to realize this. Even those who had forgotten their old faith were coming back to some form of Judaism. For this type of person, of course, a liberal service was admissible. But for the Orthodox, who had never left their customs, the new ideas were not acceptable. Both groups could not be united under one ritual. Uniformity was impossible. What was progress for one group would be retrogression for the other. Realize, said Riesser, that you cannot accomplish anything with the Orthodox. Let them alone. They do not belong to your sphere of activity. Devote your time to those who have left the faith and must be brought back. If you want our Orthodox leaders to improve the ritual which has been sanctified through martyrs' blood, then teach them through your good example. There is but one point of contact between the two groups, and that is the desire for mutual tolerance. To further this tolerance among the Orthodox will be my task, said Riesser. And that I will do this, thou good and great German man, I offer you my German handclasp!![25]

Not much of a defense was to be hoped for from Riesser. Nevertheless, help was needed. On October 18, 1818, the anniversary of Napoleon's defeat at Leipzig, the Association dedicated its temple. This was the first synagogue outside of Westphalia devoted to a Reform service. A new prayer book was introduced. The changes made were not essential, for the goal aimed at was a short and simple service. There was considerable omission. Much that was left was translated. The changes of importance occurred primarily in the musaf service where the prayers for the rebuilding of the Temple and the reestablishment of the sacrificial cult were omitted. In their place, the people asked for the gracious acceptance of prayer as a substitute for sacrifice. The prayers for the coming of the messianic kingdom were also changed where they were purely political in their significance. These last changes were dictated by expediency. The laymen who wrote this book wished to defeat the argument of those who opposed Jewish emancipation on the ground that the Jews looked forward to a restoration of their national homeland.[26]

The Orthodox of Hamburg damned the innovations of the new temple, and here again Jacobson stepped into the breach. Through his instrumentality, Eliezer Liebermann, a brilliant talmudist of very uncertain antecedents, had already been gathering responsa from various European rabbis to support the changes in the liturgy. Jacobson had, no doubt, intended to use these in defense of his own Berlin experiment, but when published, they served to defend the liberals of Hamburg.

The Hamburgers accepted the principle underlying the responsa: that they stood on good rabbinic ground; but had they not had this assurance, I do not think they would have given up their new service. They would not have admitted it, but rabbinical authority was dead for them. Here was the final and logical result of Jacobson's break with tradition almost a decade earlier in Seesen. His disciples in Hamburg, although they denied the break with the past, although they protested they were not Reformers, implied that even religious principles and institutions had to justify themselves through reason, inner worth, and a capacity to square with the times. If necessary, they were prepared to throw rabbinism as an infallible authority overboard. One of the fundamental principles of Reform was implied in this action.[27]

Jacobson's sickness did not prevent him in his well moments

from taking an interest in the work he loved so well. As early as 1817, he had introduced confirmation into the Jewish Free School in Berlin.[28] He was interested in the Association for the Culture and Science of the Jews that Zunz had established with a few choice spirits. This *Verein* was founded in the sad days of 1819, in the "Hep-Hep" period of Jewish suffering in South Germany. This group hoped "through culture and education to bring the Jews into harmonious relations with the age and the nations in which they live." Jacobson, too, was a member of this organization, but he, like his other wealthy friends, was not sufficiently interested to help it financially.[29]

The fact that a keen mind like Zunz laid so much emphasis on a proper approach to the Gentile nations should warn us not to be too severe with Jacobson, who constantly emphasized this thought. It is difficult for us in the twentieth century to realize that the generation of Jacobson and Zunz was emerging but slowly from a mediaeval past, and its fundamental problem—the one that overshadowed everything else—was a proper harmonization of the two groups and the two cultures.[30]

The following year David Caro anonymously published his *Brit Emet*. Three years before, in 1817, he had sent the manuscript to Jacobson, whom he considered one of the leading Reformers. It is not improbable that Jacobson had borne the expense of its publication.[31] Caro said that there were two chief purposes to the Mosaic law; the one was to further a belief in Divine Unity, and the other was to do away with idolatry and superstition. It was the duty of a man to help remove these superstitions. As reason developed more and more, the superstition which Moses fought would gradually disappear. Since prayer had to be understood, it might properly be recited in any language. The forms of prayer men employed had had their historical development and could, if need be, be removed. Music was not wrong; even the Psalmists had encouraged it. The organ in the service was acceptable, even though it had come from the Church. Its use would convince the Christians that Jews did not think them idolaters. Other changes should be welcomed, for they would show that Jews approved of progress, and they would help Jews work against stagnation in religious life. The rabbinate, continued Caro, needed to change its character completely. More was required of a rabbi in this age than character and a knowledge of the Talmud. The rabbi of this generation had to possess the social culture of his day, a good knowledge of Jewish affairs, secular education, and, of course, a command of the mother tongue. He had to be able to preach eloquently in the synagogue on religion, morality, biblical exegesis, homelife, education, love of fatherland, and love of humanity. After Jacobson read Caro's manuscript, he answered the author that it was a convincing presentation, but he feared that Caro would have to wear the martyr's crown because of it. Jacobson approved of everything that Caro wrote in this book.[32]

The year that Caro's *Brit Emet* was published, a branch of the Hamburg Temple was opened at Leipzig for the Spring and Autumn Fair which more or less coincided with the important Jewish holy days. Zunz and Jacob Herz Beer collaborated on the service, and Jacobson himself was very much interested. On one Atonement Day, he himself led the worship.[33]

The last ten years of his life were years of misfortune. In 1818, in his fiftieth year, he experienced a breakdown that crushed him physically and mentally.[34] From this year on, his decline was rapid. He soon ceased to be a factor of importance in the Jewish life of the time. This was unfortunate. The young Reform movement needed him badly. He could have done yeoman work in Prussia as an emancipator fighting the growing reaction which threatened Jewry. Had he retained full possession of his faculties, he might possibly have staved off the complete decay of Reform activities that came with the killing decree of 1823.

His physical condition was certainly aggravated by the death of his wife Mink, with whom he had lived a beautiful life. Jacobson, who was by no means an old man, determined to marry again. The following year, 1820, he married his nineteen-year-old niece by marriage, Jeannette, the daughter of the Hannover banker, Jacob Leffmann Cohen, and Lea Hertz Samson.[35]

He was affected by considerable financial losses, the exact character of which is not known to us. He seems to have concentrated his wealth in estates in Mecklenburg which he had purchased from the bankrupt von Moltkes and the Fluegges. Frederick Francis I of Mecklenburg-Schwerin, on March 24, 1816, granted him a patent of naturalization and the accompanying right to buy knightly estates. With these lands was bound up the privilege of sitting in the legislative assembly. The knights of the land objected to a Jew sitting with them in legislative session, but Jacobson nevertheless continued to receive invitations to appear. Later, as the political reaction manifested itself in Mecklenburg, too, Jacobson was no longer invited to attend.[36] Jacobson also had a leather factory near Potsdam and a country home at Steglitz, near Berlin. His later years were spent on his estates. Jacobson in this was consistent. He had always preached the necessity of agriculture for the Jew and spent his last years on his farms living the life of a country gentleman, although he also maintained a residence in Berlin herself.

He continued his charities to both Jew and Gentile. On his

estates in Mecklenburg, he supported schools and helped the poor and even sent money to a German Protestant congregation in Philadelphia that had appealed to him for help. It is rather strange, though, that Jacobson, before sending help, should have written to the king for permission to do so. Was this necessary? Was there a law requiring one to seek special authority from the king himself to send monies abroad? Was he trying to curry favor with the king? Was he trying to point out to the conservative Frederick William how a liberal Jew set no bounds to his charity?[37]

In 1824, Joseph Wolf, the well known educator of Dessau, now blind, came to Berlin to visit Jacobson. Jacobson had been for him a hero. Many years previously, he had dedicated his edition of the book of Micah to him with a beautiful Hebrew poem. Now he found Jacobson, though only fifty-six years of age, old, broken, and bitter against his enemies— bitter that his religious reforms had been frustrated. Wolf was moved by the intellectual decay of the man. Yet Jacobson was sufficiently himself to send Wolf a sum of money "to pay his traveling and lodging expenses," a sum that was sufficiently large to support the blind educator for quite a time.[38]

That same year, after eleven years of residence in Berlin, he became a citizen. Four years later this tragic figure died in Berlin of a hemorrhage, on the night between the 13th and the 14th of September, 1828, at the age of 60. He was interred in the Jewish cemetery in Schoenhauser Allee, not far from the grave of David Friedlaender.[39] Memorial services were held in Hamburg, Leipzig, Seesen, and even in Westphalia, the spiritual children of his striving. Salomon in Hamburg preached a memorial sermon: The truly pious one never dies. Berlin, Brunswick, and Halberstadt, cities that had benefited either materially or spiritually from his presence, ignored his passing. The differences were then too intense for them to see clearly the great good in this man. Forty years later, in 1868, Halberstadt, Brunswick, and Berlin observed the centenary of his birth. The Berliners wrote that they wished to keep in mind his fine deeds through this memorial celebration so as to encourage others to follow his example. The times had changed, people had begun to realize the intrinsic good and the sincerity of this leader. Or were the memorial services in these three cities but a courteous response to the sons who had sent a large sum of money to them all with the understanding that they divide it among the poor without regard to religious confession?[40]

His testament displayed a pious reverence for the memory of his father, a beautiful affection for his wife and children, a thoughtful consideration for his poor relatives and the servants of the house. He left 3,000 talers, a large sum in those days, for the Jewish and Christian poor of Berlin. The children who determined the apportionment sent 900 talers of this to the Jews.[41]

Now that two centuries have passed since his birth we are in a position to estimate his achievements and his influence on the history of Jewry and of Reform Judaism. Graetz says correctly that the struggle of the age was a struggle between two justified principles—a struggle to preserve Judaism in its own character and an approximation of Judaism to European culture.[42] Jacobson was one of the outstanding fighters for cultural emancipation and adjustment in Europe in the first two decades of the nineteenth century. His success was marked even in the camp of his enemies. The first attack of the Hamburg rabbis against the Temple Association was a jargon, half German, half Hebrew. The book that appeared a year later, containing the collected responsa of the Orthodox rabbis against the Reformers, had a separate section written in a tolerably good German. The very year that Frederick William III forbade German sermons in Prussia, the new Orthodox leader in Hamburg, Hakam Isaac Bernays, dressed in Protestant clerical garb and preached in German.[43]

Through the services at the Leipzig Fair, Reform made its way into the heart of Eastern European Jewry. Thousands of East European Jews came to that city and there learned of the new type of worship and carried it back home. Isaac Noah Mannheimer, one of the young preachers of the Jacobson-Beer temple, became the leader of an important congregation in Vienna in 1823 and brought the new teachings to Austria and to Hungary. Throughout all the Eastern lands the teachings of Jacobson and his associates gradually became known. People in Eastern and Central Europe began to demand a more attractive service in the synagogue with choral music and with sermon and prayer in the language of the land. Some insisted on the removal of unintelligible prayers and piyyutim from the prayer book; decorum and devotion in the service came to be seen as imperative.[44]

Jacobson strove earnestly through his compromise religious service to fight the growing indifference to the ancestral faith. He fought belligerently for political emancipation as a just right. He encouraged trade and industry and science among his fellow-Jews. A sound secular education and a proper command of the vernacular were stressed by him, not only for the average individual, but also for the rabbi and teacher. Religious education for women was for him self-understood. He strove for a type of education in Jewish life that was modern, humane, and moral in its effects.

He did not accomplish all that he intended, but he pointed the way that would have to be followed. It was a notable contribution of his to Jewish life that he first helped kill the idea that a Jewish synagogue was synonymous with disorder. It was primarily through him that good taste, simplicity, refinement came back into the Jewish service. These are all externals, to be sure, but they are indispensable in a truly religious life.

The type of service that he developed in Seesen and Berlin spread to Hamburg and ultimately far beyond Germany—to North America. The Hamburgers realized that they were following in the footsteps of Jacobson, for they dedicated their first prayer book to him and acknowledged in three pages of florid thanks their great spiritual debt to him. They expressed the hope that he would live to see his "work spreading itself more and more throughout Israel."[45]

Jacobson and his friends influenced young intellectuals. Young men began to prepare themselves for the professions of teacher and preacher. Quite a number of those who were active in the religious life of the next generation were trained by Jacobson. Through these men and through his own efforts, the modern tendencies made themselves felt all through Europe. The successful attempt on the part of stubborn traditionalists to frustrate the harmonization of Judaism and the modern state in Jacobson's own time was impossible, however, after his death, as the second generation of nineteenth-century youth grew up. It was this generation, whether Reform or Orthodox, that proved the wisdom of many of Jacobson's purposes.[46]

The creation of an attractive ritual may have marked the limit of his religious accomplishments, but not of his ambitions. He had hoped through his reforms not merely to beautify Jewish life outwardly, but also to enrich it inwardly. It must be admitted, however, that this ideal was rather vague in his mind. It is unfortunate that he did not emphasize this line of thought. Although he was truly a religious man, religion was not the all-consuming fire in his bosom.

Jacobson's most vital mistake was his failure to realize that Judaism could not live only through a broad system of morals, but also needed the sustenance of a strong inner religious sentiment and a deep knowledge of Jewish life and literature.

His revisions of Jewish custom and ceremonial presuppose certain definite theological principles at variance with the Orthodox masses, yet basic for the new Reform movement in Judaism. In his theory of Judaism he was a Reform Jew. He broke intellectually with the past; emotionally he could not. Others fought his battles in the coming generation. He introduced the issue betwen Reform and Orthodoxy, between Liberalism and Authority. His actions demanded a clarification of concepts. Practically all the great works of Zunz would attempt to justify the new attitudes historically. The polemics of the first two decades of the century had made it essential to undertake a scientific study of the principles and traditions of Judaism.[47]

Abbreviations

AZJ   *Allgemeine Zeitung des Judenthums*
JJGL   *Jahrbuch fuer juedische Geschichte und Literatur*
MGWJ   *Monatsschrift fuer Geschichte und Wissenschaft des Juden-*
           tums
ZGJD   *Zeitschrift fuer die Geschichte der Juden in Deutschland*
Zunz, GV   L. Zunz, *Die gottesdienstlichen Vortraege der Juden.*
           Frankfort on the Main, 1892

Bibliography

Arnheim, J. *Die Jacobson-Schule.* 2d ed. Brunswick, 1867.

Arnheim, J. *Bericht ueber die Jacobson-Schule.* Hanover, 1871.

Aub, Joseph. *Predigt . . . bei der Feier des hundertjaehrigen Geburtstages Israel Jacobsons.* Berlin, 1868.

Auerbach, B. H. *Geschichte der israelitischen Gemeinde Halberstadt.* Halberstadt, 1866.

Auerbach, L. *Das Judenthum und seine Bekenner in Preussen.* Berlin, 1890.

Baerwald, H., and S. Adler. "Geschichte der Realschule . . . zu Frankfurt am Main, 1804-1904," *Philanthropin . . . Festschrift.* Frankfort on the Main, 1904.

Baerwald, H., and M. Isler, "Briefe von Lazarus und Gabriel Riesser," *ZGJD,* I (1887), 366-76.

Bemerkungen ueber des Herrn Geh. Finanzraths Israel Jakobsohn Unterthaenigste Vorstellung an . . . den Fuerst Primas der Rheinischen Confoederation. Frankfort on the Main, 1808.

Berliner, M. *Stammbaum der Samsonschen Familie.* 3d ed. Hanover, 1912.

Bernfeld, S. *Toledot Ha-riformatzion Ha-datit Beyisrael.* 2d ed. Warsaw, 1923.

Bran, A. *Gesammelte Actenstuecke ueber die Verbesserung des Zustandes der Juden.* Hamburg, 1806-1807.

Cambridge Modern History. Vol. IX. New York, 1906.

Cohen, M. "Unsere Familien Chronik," *JJGL,* XII (1909), 110-34.

Doering, H. "Israel Jacobson," *Allgemeine Encyclopaedie der Wissenschaften und Kuenste,* eds. J. S. Ersch and J. G. Gruber, XIV^2 (1837), 18-19.

Donath, L. *Geschichte der Juden in Mecklenburg.* Leipzig, 1874.

Dubnow, S. M. *Die Neueste Geschichte des Juedischen Volkes.* Vols. I-II. Berlin, 1920.

Elbogen, Ismar. *Der juedische Gottesdienst in seiner geschichtlichen Entwickelung. Leipzig,* 1913. [Notes to the 2d ed. have been used.]

Eleh dibre habrit. Altona, 1819.

Enelow, H. G. "The President's Message," *Central Conference of Amerian Rabbis Yearbook,* XXXVIII (1928), 163-95.

Feder, E. B. *Israelitischer Ehrentempel.* Dinkelsbuehl, 1840.

Fisher, H. A. L. *Studies in Napoleonic Statesmanship: Germany.* Oxford, 1903.

Franke, K. *Die Kulturwerte der deutschen Literatur.* Vol. II. Berlin, 1923.

Freund, I. *Die Emanzipation der Juden in Preussen.* Vols. I-II. Berlin, 1912.

Friedland, N. *Zur Geschichte des Tempels der Jacobsonschule.* Seesen, 1910.

[Friedrich, G.] *Die Juden und ihre Gegner.* Frankfort on the Main, 1816.

Geiger, L. "Die Juden und die deutsche Literatur: Goethe und die Juden," *ZGJD,* I (1887), 321-58.

Geiger, L. *Geschichte der Juden in Berlin.* Vols. I-II. Berlin, 1871.

Geitel, G. A. *Gesuch . . . an . . . Herrn Herzog Wilhelm von Braunschweig-Lueneburg* [etc.]. Brunswick, 1831.

Graetz, H. *Geschichte der Juden,* ed. M. Brann. Vol. XI. 2d ed. Leipzig, 1900.

Halphen, A. E. *Recueil des Lois.* Paris, 1851.

Heine, Heinrich. *Briefwechsel,* ed. F. Hirth. Vol. I. Munich and Berlin, 1914.

Heinemann, J. "Das israelitische Konsistorium im . . . Koenigreiche Westphalen . . . 1808-1813," *Allgemeines Archiv des Judenthums* (*Jedidja, neue Folge*), III (No. 1—1843), 1-70.

Henne-Am Rhyn, O. *Kulturgeschichte des Judentums.* Jena, 1880.

Herrmann, M. *Lebensgeschichte des Peter Beer.* Prague, 1839.

Heussi, K. *Kompendium der Kirchengeschichte.* 5th ed. Tuebingen, 1922.

Horwitz, L. *Die Israeliten unter dem Koenigreich Westfalen.* Berlin, 1900.

Horwitz, L. "Neue Beitraege zur Geschichte und Taetigkeit des koeniglich westphaelischen Konsistoriums der Israeliten zu Kassel, 1807-1815," *MGWJ,* LIII (1909), 513-24, 723-35.

Horwitz, L. "Zur Charakteristik Israel Jacobsons," *AZJ,* LXVIII (1904), 391-93.

Jacobson, Israel. *Les premiers pas de la nation juive vers le bonheur sous les auspices du grand Monarque Napoléon.* Paris, 1806.

Jacobson, Israel. *Rede am Dankfeste wegen des den Juden erteilten Buergerrechts.* Brunswick, 1808.

Jacobson, Israel. *Rede bei der Feier der Geburt eines Enkels des Durchlauchtigsten Herzogs von Braunschweig-Lueneburg.* 1804.

Jacobson, Israel. *Rede bei Eroeffnung des Koeniglich Westphaelischen Consistoriums der Israeliten.* Cassel, 1808.

Jacobson, Israel. "Rede des Herrn Praesidenten [bei Einweihung des Jakobstempels zu Seesen, 1810]," *Sulamith,* III, No. 1 (1810), 303-17.

Jacobson, Israel. *Rede des Praesidenten Jacobsohn bei der von ihm Sabbats den 8 Nissan 5572 in der hiesigen Synagoge verrichteten Konfirmation.* Cassel, 1812.

Jacobson, Israel. *Unterthaenigste Vorstellung an Seine Hoheit den Fuerst Primas der Rheinischen Konfoederation ueber Hoechstdessen neue Staedtigkeits- und Schutzordnung fuer die Judenschaft in Frankfurt am Main.* Brunswick, 1808.

Jost, I. M. *Allgemeine Geschichte des Israelitischen Volkes.* Vol. II. Berlin, 1832.

Jost, I. M. *Geschichte der Israeliten.* Vol. IX. Berlin, 1828.

Jost, I. M. *Geschichte des Judenthums.* Leipzig, 1850.

Jost, I. M. "Jacobson und die neuern Richtungen," *Israelitische Annalen,* I (Nos. 29-31—1839).

Jost, I. M. "Lazarus Bendavid," *Freitagabend* (Frankfort on the Main, 1859), pp. 189-91.

Jost, I. M. *Neuere Geschichte der Israeliten von 1815 bis 1845.* Berlin, 1846-1847.

Jost, I. M. "Vor einem halben Jahrhundert," *Sippurim,* ed. Wolf Pascheles, III (6th ed.; Prague, 1883), 141-65.

Kernholt, O. *Vom Ghetto zur Macht.* Leipzig, 1921.

Kleinschmidt, A. "Dr. Israel Jacobson," *Zeitschrift des Harzvereins,* XXIII (1890), 202-12.

Kleinschmidt, A. *Geschichte des Koenigreichs Westfalen.* Gotha, 1893.

Koehler, M. *Die Juden in Halberstadt und Umgebung bis zur Emanzipation.* Berlin, 1927.

Kohut, A. *Gekroente und Ungekroente Judenfreunde.* Berlin, 1913.

Lazarus, F. *Das koeniglich westphaelische Konsistorium der Israeliten.* Pressburg, 1914.

Lesser, L. *Chronik der Gesellschaft der Freunde in Berlin.* Berlin, 1842.

Lewinsky, A. "Israel Jacobsons Vater," *AZJ,* LXVII (1903), 557-59.

Liebe, G. *Das Judentum.* Leipzig, 1903.

Liepmannssohn, S. L. *Aufruf zu einer Synagogen-Feier und Errichtung eines Ehrengedaechtnisses fuer Israel Jacobson.* Horn, 1868.

Lippmann, N. *Leben und Wirken des . . . David Caro.* Glogau, 1840.

Maenss, J. "Die Juden im Koenigreich Westfalen," *Geschichts-Blaetter fuer Stadt und Land Magdeburg,* XLII (1907), 47-66.

Maybaum, S. "Aus dem Leben von Leopold Zunz," *Lehranstalt fuer die Wissenschaft des Judenthums in Berlin: Bericht XII.* Berlin, 1894.

Paulsen, F. *German Education*. Translated by T. Lorenz. New York, 1908.

Philippson, E. *Israel Jacob*. Goslar, 1903.

Philippson, M. *Neueste Geschichte des juedischen Volkes*. Vol. I. 2d ed. Frankfort on the Main, 1922.

Philippson, P. *Biographische Skizzen*. Leipzig, 1864-1866.

Philipson, D. *The Reform Movement in Judaism*. New York, 1907.

Ritter, I. H. *David Friedlaender*. Berlin, 1861.

Roenne, L. von, and H. Simon. *Die frueheren und gegenwaertigen Verhaeltnisse der Juden in den saemmtlichen Landestheilen des preussischen Staates*. Breslau, 1843.

Rosenstock, M. *Festschrift zur hundertjaehrigen Jubelfeier der Samsonschule*. Wolfenbuettel, 1886.

Ruelf, G. "Einiges aus der ersten Zeit und ueber den Stifter der Jacobson-Schule," *Juedisches Litteratur-Blatt,* XVIII (Nos. 45-52—1889) and XIX (Nos. 1-2—1890).

Salkover, M. "The Assembly of Notables and Sanhedrin convened by Napoleon the First." Unpublished rabbinical thesis, Hebrew Union College, 1919.

Salomon, G. *Auswahl von Predigten . . . fuer Israeliten*. Dessau, 1818.

Schnee, Heinrich, *Die Hoffinanz und der moderne Staat: Geschichte und System der Hoffaktoren an deutschen Fuerstenhoefen im Zeitalter des Absolutismus*. Vols. I-V. Berlin, 1953-1965.

Schottlaender, B. *Sendschreiben an meine Brueder die Israeliten in Westfalen*. Brunswick, 1808.

Seligmann, C. *Geschichte der Juedischen Reform-Bewegung*. Frankfort on the Main, 1922.

Silberstein, S. "Das Testament Israel Jacobsons," *JJGL,* XXVIII (1927), 100-109.

Silberstein, S. "Zur Vorgeschichte der Judenemanzipation in Mecklenburg," *AZJ,* LXXVII (1913), 104-5.

Steinhardt, M. *Dibre Iggeret*. Roedelheim, 1812.

Steinhausen, G. *Kulturgeschichte der Deutschen in der Neuzeit*. 2d ed. Leipzig, 1918.

Stendhal, Henri. "Diary: 1807-1808" (excerpt), *AZJ,* LXXXIV (1920), 108.

Stern, A. "Hundert Jahre im Dienst des religioesen Fortschritts," *AZJ,* LXXIV (1910), 511-12.

Stern, S. *Geschichte des Judenthums*. Frankfort on the Main, 1857.

Strodtmann, A. *H. Heines Leben und Werke*. Vol. I. 2d ed. Berlin, 1873.

Strombeck, F. C. von. "Darstellungen aus meinem Leben und aus meiner Zeit," *AZJ,* I (1837), 292.

Sulamith. Vols. I-IX. 1806-1846.

Tama, D. *Organisation civile et religieuse des Israélites.* Paris, 1808.

Thilly, F. A. *A History of Philosophy.* New York, 1914.

Windelband, W. *Lehrbuch der Geschichte der Philosophie,* ed. E. Rothacker. 9th-10th ed. Tuebingen, 1921.

Witte, K. *Israel; oder, der edle Jude.* Leipzig, 1805.

Zimmermann, P. "Israel Jacobson," *Braunschweigisches Magazin* (September-October, 1906). There is a slightly revised edition of this address in *Brunsvicensia Judaica.* Brunswick, 1966, pp. 23-42.

Zirndorf, H. *Isaak Marcus Jost.* Cincinnati, 1886.

Zuckermann, M. *Kollektanea zur Geschichte der Juden in Hannoverland.* Hanover, 1912.

Zunz, L. *Die Gottesdienstlichen Vortraege der Juden,* ed. N. Bruell. 2d ed. Frankfort on the Main, 1892.

Zunz, L. *Predigten gehalten in der neuen Israelitischen Synagoge zu Berlin.* Berlin, 1823.

Zunz, L. *Samuel Meyer Ehrenberg.* Brunswick, 1854.

Notes

JACOBSON'S BACKGROUND

1. Jost, who knew Jacobson well, treated of him in some detail in his *Allgemeine Geschichte,* pp. 511 ff.; *Geschichte des Judenthums,* pp. 233 ff.; *Neuere Geschichte,* I, 25 ff.; III, 14 ff.; *Gesch. der Israeliten,* pp. 138 ff. His treatment, upon which all others are founded, was sympathetic and just, at times even apologetic in tone. Stern, *Geschichte des Judenthums,* pp. 155 ff., was sympathetic and brilliant in his interpretation. His work, though little known, has been drawn on heavily by Jewish historians. Graetz, XI, 238 ff., was bitter, at times unjust, and even inaccurate. Yet he was always keen and incisive with a magnificent appreciation of historic values. He is, after all, the great master. Kleinschmidt, "Dr. Israel Jacobson," treated him briefly and coldly, almost antipathetically. He followed Graetz in his interpretation of purely Jewish activities.

David Philipson's account in *Reform Movement in Judaism,* pp. 17 ff., limits itself primarily to a study of the religious contribution of the man. It is a sympathetic presentation. Dubnow, I, 212 ff.; II, 69 ff., is very brief and unsympathetic. The same may be said of Martin Philippson, I, 27 ff. This distaste for Jacobson was one thing these two historians had in common. Zimmermann, "Israel Jacobson," treated in detail his life in relation to the Duchy of Brunswick and the Kingdom of Westphalia. It is a full and interesting and very fair treatment. Seligmann, pp. 68 ff., presents a short but very fine study of Jacobson as a religionist. Elbogen, pp. 398 ff., gives a very good evaluation of Jacobson. A general criticism that I wish to apply to all these works which treat of the religious ideas of Jacobson is that they do not go far enough. They judge the man solely on the ground of what he actually did, not on the basis of what he thought and wanted to do. He succeeded only in reforming the Jewish religious service and some customs. Had he dared, he would have gone further and cut deeper.

2. Cf. Thilly, p. 383; *The Education of Henry Adams* (Boston, 1918), p. 458.

3. Cf. Koehler, "Vorwort" and "Ergebnisse"; cf. also Auerbach, *Geschichte der israelitischen Gemeinde Halberstadt.*

4. Windelband, p. 416; Salomon on *Aufklaerung* in *Sulamith,* II, No. 1, pp. 217 ff.; Schottlaender, *Sendschreiben,* p. 7.

5. Franke, p. 456; Thilly, pp. 382 ff.; "Deism," *Jewish Encyclopedia.*

6. Herder, *Saemmtliche Werke,* Part 10, p. 117, quoted in Friedrich, p. 32.

7. Herder, *Ideen zur Philosophie und Geschichte der Menschheit,* IV, 41, quoted in Geitel, p. 10.

8. Steinhausen, pp. 54-129; Heussi, pp. 326-97; Windelband, pp. 408-48.

YOUTH

1. I question very much if the father, had he been living, would have approved of the service introduced in Seesen.

2. Witte was a personal friend of Jacobson for many years. He was an unusual fellow, and I suspect that in his life of Israel Jacob he did not follow the strait and narrow path of historical accuracy. Jost tells us that he once found himself at the dinner table with Jacobson, Bendavid, and Witte. The pastor said he once saw spirits. Bendavid, the true rationalist, interrupted: "Pastor, did you really see them with your own eyes?" "Surely," he answered, "otherwise I wouldn't say so." "That's nice," answered Bendavid, "for if I had seen them I wouldn't have believed it." Jost, "Lazarus Bendavid," p. 191.

3. This type of generous giving influenced his youthful son, the subject of this work. The following anecdote was related by a youthful friend of Israel Jacobson. The ten-year-old child had asked his father for a savings box and was given one. In the course of time, he accumulated over 150 talers. After a while, the father asked about it, for he wished to add something. However, when the box was brought to him, he found an account in it showing that all the monies had been expended. The ten-year-old lad had bought wood for the poor of Halberstadt! (Hildesheimer *Sonntagsblatt,* 1832, No. 22, pp. 183 ff., quoted in *AZJ,* LXVII, 558).

4. Auerbach, *Halberstadt,* pp. 138-39; Kleinschmidt, "Jacobson," p. 202; Zimmermann, p. 97.

I have used the edition of Witte published in Leipzig, 1805, by Heinrich Graeff. It is called *Israel; oder, der edle Jude: eine wahre Geschichte von Karl Witte.* An engraving of the father is given with the dates: 14th April, 1729-25th November, 1803. The following verse is also given:

"Behold an Israelite in whose heart there is no guile" (cf. John 1:47). There is another edition used by E. Philippson, "Israel

Jacob." This first (?) edition was published in 1804 by Friedrich Wilh. Nettling.

5. Graetz, p. 287, has, wrongly, 1769. This Graetz secured from *Sulamith,* II, No. 1, p. 31, which is in error in placing his birth in 1769. Donath, pp. 179 ff., speaks of a brother of Jacobson. I have nowhere else found that Jacobson had either brothers or sisters. Jacobson's father was named Israel Jacob. Jacobson took the name Israel Jakobssohn or Jacobssohn. But in accordance with the decree of March 31, 1808, requiring Jews to assume definite names, he finally settled on Israel Jacobson (*Sulamith,* II, No. 1, pp. 30, 170). But even afterwards the name Jakobsohn and other variants are found (cf. *AZJ,* LXX, 186).

6. Jost, *Annalen,* p. 226.

7. Steinhardt, *Dibre Iggeret,* Question No. 1; Jost, *Judenthum,* pp. 322-23; *Sulamith,* VIII, No. 1, pp. 279-80; Jost, *Neuere Geschichte,* p. 139; Graetz, XI, 288 ff.; Jost, *Allgemeine Geschichte,* p. 533; Arnheim, *Jacobson-Schule,* pp. 2-3; Kleinschmidt, "Jacobson," p. 202; Zimmermann, p. 98.

BRUNSWICK

1. Mink (Menckel or Minna) Herz Samson married Israel Jacobson in 1786. She was born on the 17th of October, 1766, and died on February 4, 1819. She bore him six children. The extremely interesting family tree of Jacobson may be found in Berliner, *Stammbaum,* Table 6. Many of the descendants intermarried into aristocratic German and English families. The Jacobsonians in this table are found all the way from London to East India. Unless otherwise specified, the material for Brunswick is taken from Ruelf and Zimmermann.

2. Herz Samson died on December 12, 1794, and Jacobson was appointed *Kammeragent* on the 30th of December, 1794, and the 5th of January, 1795. He was appointed *Landesrabbiner* on January 1, 1795. The Weser District comprises the present areas of Gandersheim and Holzminden (Lazarus, p. 10).

3. *Sulamith,* VII, No. 2, pp. 39 ff.; Jost, *Gesch. der Israeliten,* pp. 140-41.

4. The Jewish Free School of Berlin was founded in 1778; the Royal William School in Breslau in 1791; the Ducal Franz School in Dessau in 1799.

5. The Mendelssohnian Pentateuch translation was completed in 1783, and the Samson Free School was opened in 1807. It was in this same year, too, that the Westphalian kingdom, which granted the Jews citizenship, was established.

6. Letter to Staatsrat von Hennings, in Seligmann, pp. 50-51.

7. Arnheim, *Jacobson-Schule,* pp. 2-3.

8. Graetz, XI, 234.

9. *Sulamith,* III, No. 1, pp. 303 ff.; VII, No. 2, pp. 39 ff.; Stern, *Geschichte,* pp. 160-61, 163, 174; Kleinschmidt, "Jacobson," pp. 203-4; Paulsen, *German Education;* Friedland, *Zur Geschichte;* Geitel, pp. 33 ff.; Arnheim, *Jacobson-Schule,* pp. 9 ff.; Lazarus, p. 12; Zunz, *GV,* pp. 465, 469.

10. Zimmermann, p. 98; Auerbach, *Halberstadt,* p. 149.

11. Kleinschmidt, "Jacobson," p. 203.

12. The school building was purchased on March 16, 1801. On the 3rd of July, he and the Jewish teachers of the school were given certain civil rights. In October, the students came in.

13. Jacobson had quite a reputation as a Jewish educator, not only because of his establishment of the school at Seesen, but also through his reorganization of the Samson Free School at Wolfenbuettel and by reason of his support of the Frankfort Philanthropinum and other schools. Toward the end of 1805, Jacobson helped Isaac Herz Samson, his brother-in-law, reorganize the two Samson talmudic schools at Wolfenbuettel. Out of this reorganization came the Samson Free School, a modern institution. This was in April, 1807. Like the Seesen school, it was to be an elementary school and *Realschule* for poor Jewish children. They were here to be prepared for agricultural work, trade, and business. The better minds were to be sent to the higher schools. Jost and Zunz were among the fortunate who received a higher education. This school soon surpassed the Seesen institution, which was never in Jacobson's time really outstanding. Kleinschmidt, "Jacobson," p. 205; *Sulamith,* I, No. 1, p. 491; No. 2, pp. 49 ff.; Geitel, p. 34; Jost, *Gesch. der Israeliten,* pp. 142 ff.; Rosenstock, pp. 13 ff.; Stern, *Geschichte,* pp. 160-61, 174; Zunz, *GV,* pp. 465, 469; Baerwald and Adler, p. 29.

14. This estimate is made on an admitted income of 30,000 talers. Stendhal said he had two millions. If he meant francs, this would have been a fortune of about half a million talers.

15. On the 26th of February, 1803, he was appointed a *Commerzienrath* by Hesse-Darmstadt. On the 7th of March, 1803, he was appointed *Hofagent* by Baden, and on the 2nd of June, 1806, he was given his highest title by Mecklenburg-Schwerin: *Geheimer Finanzrath.* This is the title by which he is usually known (*Sulamith,* I, No. 1, p. 92).

16. Auerbach, *Halberstadt,* p. 139.

17. The French administrator sent into Brunswick this year, 1806, was misinformed or misunderstood when he said that Jacobson was a

member of the Council of State. The Frenchman said: ". . . at a time when the Jews were shamefully persecuted in Germany, he [the Duke] placed a merchant named Jacobson on his Council of State, a devout Jew, but a virtuous man and a philanthropist." Fisher, p. 137.

18. On May 28, 1805, he received for himself and descendants the civil rights of Brunswick (Kleinschmidt, "Jacobson," pp. 203-4). I cannot determine how this privilege differed from the one accorded in February, 1804, or in July, 1801, in Seesen. All three seem to grant complete rights of citizenship, unless they were only municipal rights.

19. B. Schottlaender to Trenell, Oct. 12, 1806 (MSS, Jewish National and University Library, Jerusalem).

20. *Sulamith*, VII, No. 2, pp. 39 ff.; Jost, *Gesch. der Israeliten*, pp. 140-41. There seems to be confusion as to whether the name of Jacobson's rival was a Nathan Jacob or an Israel Nathan who carried on his business under the title of Nathan Jacob, Jr.

21. Arnheim, *Bericht*, pp. 10-14; *Jacobson-Schule*, pp. 11-13.

22. This letter, like much of the material presented here, is found in Ruelf.

23. Lazarus, p. 11.

24. Jacobson made his demands on the duke on June 20, 1806.

25. Strombeck, p. 292.

26. Schottlaender to Trenell, Oct. 12, 1806.

27. The *Leibzoll* was removed in his own land: Brunswick-Wolfenbuettel, April 23, 1803. Lazarus Riesser, the father of Gabriel Riesser, wrote a poem in honor of Jacobson because he had effected the abolition of this tax in Brunswick in 1803 (*ZGJD*, I [1887], 366). In Baden, the tax was abolished on January 20, 1804. Wolf Breidenbach did even more than Jacobson to remove these tolls in various parts of Germany. *Sulamith*, VIII, No. 2, p. 369; Graetz, XI, 238; "Leibzoll," *Jewish Encyclopedia*.

28. Jacobson, *Unter. Vorstellung*, pp. 3-4.

29. This letter is contained in Jacobson, *Premiers Pas*, which I have not been able to examine, though I have used the extracts in Bran.

30. Jacobson, *Premiers Pas*. I have not been able to determine the chronology or the exact contents of the three writings of Jacobson in this episode: the letter to Napoleon, the memorial brought by Schottlaender to Paris, and the *Premiers Pas*. The letter was probably the first communication. This was probably followed by the *Premiers Pas*, which was published after the decree of May 30, 1806, and before September 18, 1806, for on this latter day Mole publicly announced the convening of the Sanhedrin, of which Jacobson in the book knew

nothing. It may have been published as early as June or July, the month that saw the formation of the Rhine Confederation. Either the memorial brought by Schottlaender or the *Premiers Pas* was widely known in France by the 26th of July, 1806. Tama, p. 125, says that a writing of Jacobson was at this time widely known. From Schottlaender's letters, we know that he left Paris in late August or early September, 1806, on his way back home. Letter to "Nini," his fiancée, dated Fast of Gedaliah, 5567 (15th of September, 1806). The memorial on education was probably submitted by him in person to the Assembly in July or August. Schottlaender complained bitterly at first of the treatment accorded him by the Assembly (letter to Trenell, October 12, 1806). In a later letter, he is pleased that the Assembly has followed his advice in some things (letter to Trenell, December 27, 1806). It may be that Schottlaender's memorial and the *Premiers Pas* are identical, for both deal with education.

31. Stern, *Geschichte*, pp. 193-94.

32. Zimmermann, "Jacobson," p. 104; Stern, *Geschichte,* p. 150; Graetz, XI, 289. Lazarus, pp. 11-12, is of the opinion that Schottlaender wrote this appeal for Jacobson. Possibly he did, but I believe the ideas to be those of Jacobson. The boldness and vigor of proposed action are typically Jacobsonian. In view of his limited secular education, it is not improbable that someone, probably Schottlaender, as the Halberstadters suspected, corrected and polished his writings (cf. Auerbach, *Halberstadt,* p. 150).

33. Stern, *Geschichte,* p. 163; Lazarus, pp. 11-12. This is probably the significance of the statement in *Unter. Vorstellung,* p. 4, where Jacobson states that he has lifted up his voice before the throne of Napoleon and it has been heard. Salkover is also of the opinion that the *Premiers Pas* of Jacobson influenced Napoleon in the calling of a Sanhedrin. Napoleon, says Salkover, learned of the power of the Sanhedrin, as the supreme Jewish tribunal, from this work. He may have desired to establish such a court in order to dominate not only French, but all European Jewry.

34. There is a good analysis of this decree in Fisher, p. 316.

35. Jost, *Neuere Geschichte,* I, 24-25.

36. *Unter. Vorstellung* appeared in French translation as *Très Humble Remontrance* [etc.] (Brunswick, 1808). The *Unter. Vorstellung* was dated Brunswick, January 24, 1808 (cf. Kleinschmidt, "Jacobson," p. 206).

37. Jost, *Neuere Geschichte,* I, 24-25.

38. *Bemerkungen.* Evidently before April, 1808, for on April 3, 1808,

Goethe had read it and wrote to Bettina von Arnim about it.

39. The pun is evident. Letter to Bettina von Arnim, April 20, 1808 (Geiger in *ZGJD*, I [1887], 331 ff.).

40. Letter to Bettina von Arnim, April 3, 1808.

41. Kleinschmidt, "Jacobson," p. 203.

42. Graetz thought so: XI, 289. So did the anti-Semite Kernholt, p. 75; Henne-Am-Rhyn, p. 444.

43. Kleinschmidt, "Jacobson," p. 206.

44. Friedland, p. 7.

45. For details, cf. Ruelf, XVIII, No. 52; XIX, Nos. 1-2.

46. Zimmermann, p. 105.

47. *Sulamith,* VII, No. 2, pp. 39 ff.

48. *Cambridge Modern History,* IX, 411-12; Philippson, *Neueste Geschichte,* I, 30.

49. Ruelf, XIX, No. 2.

50. This description is based on the picture, undated, in Arnheim, *Jacobson-Schule.* The picture on the first page of *Sulamith,* II, No. 1, is softer. Much more than the above, it gives the impression of a rather pompous, naive, good-natured individual. Yet strength is written all over the face. The round skullcap here is large, completely covering the head as far as the ears, where the abundant curls again come into evidence.

51. Zirndorf, p. 105.

52. The above account of Jacobson is based on material found in the various books already quoted or to be quoted. I have drawn much from Jost's *Annalen.* The notes of Stendhal are taken from his 1807-1808 German impressions.

WESTPHALIA

1. Arnheim, *Jacobson-Schule,* p. 5; Zimmermann, p. 105.

2. Lazarus, p. 76, Note 1.

3. Cf. Graetz, XI, 287.

4. *Sulamith,* I, No. 2, last page.

5. A picture of this medal may be seen in the *Encyclopaedia Judaica* (Berlin, 1928), I, 576; *Jewish Encyclopedia,* I, 123. Cf. also *Sulamith,* II, No. 1, p. 30.

6. Kleinschmidt, *Westfalen,* p. 22.

7. Cohen in *JJGL.*

8. Friedrich, pp. 22-28.

9. Zunz, *GV,* p. 465.

10. Cf. Halphen, p. 38.

11. Horwitz, *Westfalen,* pp. 8 ff.; Heinemann, pp. 9 ff.; Lazarus, p. 6.

12. Heinemann, p. 10.

13. *Ibid.,* p. 63.

14. *Sulamith,* III, No. 1, p. 13.

15. This grouping of Jewish law is found in Ibn Daud's *Emunah Ramah.*

16. Heinemann, p. 61.

17. Jost, *Allgemeine Geschichte,* pp. 511-12.

18. Auerbach, *Halberstadt,* p. 139.

19. This was the second thanksgiving service for the conferring of political equality. The first was held in January (*Sulamith,* VIII, No. 1, pp. 279-80).

20. Horwitz, *Westfalen,* p. 12.

21. The law establishing the consistory is in *Sulamith,* II, No. 1, pp. 3 ff. The law was prepared probably by Jacobson and approved by the authorities (Horwitz, *Westfalen,* p. 19). In a way it is a partial realization of the program that Jacobson laid down about two years before this in his *Premiers Pas.*

22. Schottlaender, *Sendschreiben,* appeared also in a Hebrew translation in *Meassef,* 1809, p. 9. Schottlaender now called himself Schott, although occasionally the older name persists.

23. Jacobson, *Unter. Vorstellung,* pp. 6-7.

24. *Sulamith,* II, No. 1, p. 10.

25. Heinemann, pp. 103-4.

26. All this in a letter of Friedlaender to Aaron Wolfssohn sent from Berlin to Brunswick, September 21, 1808 (Lazarus, p. 17).

27. Heinemann, p. 104.

28. *Sulamith,* II, No. 1, p. 10.

29. In fact, he is really directly responsible for almost every act of the Westphalian consistory during the period of its life, 1808-1813, and his career cannot be judged apart from his work in this organization.

30. Jacobson had offered an appointment to the elder Heinemann and the father of the Halberstadt Auerbach, but they refused to come because of their Orthodox leanings. Heinemann's letter of refusal is found in *Allgemeines Archiv des Judenthums,* II (1842), 369 ff. Peter Beer, invited to be a Lay-Councillor, refused because he did not wish to leave his own land and because he had no confidence in the future of Westphalia (Herrmann, p. 20). Samuel Meyer Ehrenberg, Zunz's friend and teacher, also was invited to become a member of the consistory. He refused because he wished to devote himself to his teaching

at Wolfenbuettel, and because he thought his position there surer and more independent. Jacobson was hurt by this refusal, yet responded to the invitation of Ehrenberg to come and inspect the school. He came, unannounced, and examined the children very thoroughly. They passed a good examination, and as he left he called out to Ehrenberg: "Don't let even the Devil himself take you away from this place" (Zunz, *Ehrenberg*, p. 24).

31. Lazarus, pp. 23 ff. Graetz, XI, 290, is wrong in his judgment of this man.

32. Lazarus, pp. 21 ff.

33. Fraenkel was the editor of *Sulamith,* the first German Jewish newspaper. Published first in Dessau, it was moved to Cassel for a time when its editor was made Lay-Councillor there. As early as 1807, Fraenkel writes of the need for good schools, free education for children, teachers' colleges, and the like *(Sulamith,* I, No. 2, pp. 41 ff.). In the winter of 1807, while still in Dessau, he wrote an essay in his paper on the position of the Jews in ancient and modern times. His ideas are of interest. He says: Let us get away from petty trade. Let us accept the influence of the idea of humanity. We are not Orientals any more. There is only one true Jewish religion. Away with the slack. Do not emphasize minor ceremonies. The fundamental ideas have been neglected. This ceremonial and mythical Judaism drives away the educated Jew. Let us have a uniform Jewish liturgy. The one now employed by the Oriental Jews is the best, not the Polish and German ritual. Let us have decorum in the services, orderly reading of the prayers, good Hebrew, and a good knowledge of the vernacular. He appeals to the wise Jacobson to help improve the devotion in the synagogues. He asks for good schools and attacks the talmudic prebends. Good schools will solve the problem of Jewish atheism. Better community organization is necessary, also better charitable organizations. The business of early burials must be stopped *(Sulamith,* I, No. 2, pp. 353 ff.). All this above before Jacobson was a power in Westphalia. I am very much of the opinion that Fraenkel was a strong influence on Jacobson, particularly in the matter of Jewish education in Westphalia. Fraenkel, Kalkar, and Heinemann were in charge of the Department of Education (Lazarus, p. 34).

34. Horwitz, *Westfalen,* p. 20.

35. Jacobson was not fond of the word Jew. He preferred the words Israelite and Mosaite.

36. Horwitz, *Westfalen,* p. 24.

37. *Ibid.,* p. 27.

38. Halphen, pp. 37 ff.

39. *Sulamith,* II, No. 2, pp. 300 ff.; Horwitz, *Westfalen,* p. 27.

40. It is possible that here Jacobson is referring to his *Premiers Pas,* which calls for a reorganization of the Jewish religious group and resulted, possibly, in the ultimate establishment of the French consistory.

41. Horwitz, *Westfalen,* pp. 49 ff.

42. *Ibid.,* pp. 41 ff.

43. *Ibid.,* pp. 75-76.

44. See below for the Confession of Faith. The implication in his letter seems, however, that the state may well refuse his request, for in matters of dispute that do not involve spiritual concepts, the state is supreme. In any event, Jacobson refused to take a positive stand.

45. Letter to Hardenberg, Feb. 14, 1811 (Freund, II, 428).

46. Freund, I, 166. In the *Denkwuerdigkeiten von Heinrich und Amalie v. Beguelin aus den Jahren 1807-1813,* edited by A. Ernst (Berlin, 1892), pp. 290 ff., Amalie states that Hardenberg was once in need of money because of his separation from his first wife. He was expected to return her fortune. Unasked for, a Jew lent him money at a low rate of interest. The Chancellor never forgot this courtesy and helped the Jews in Prussia when they fought for civil equality. Freund, I, 165-66, is of the opinion that Israel Jacobson is the man who came to the rescue of Hardenberg. A writer in the *Mittheilungen a. d. Verein z. Abwehr d. Antisem.* (1912), p. 127, is of the opinion that the Jew in question was Herz Samson, the father-in-law of Jacobson.

47. Letter to Hardenberg, Feb. 14, 1811 (Freund, II, 428). Letter sent from Berlin, where Jacobson had gone to speak to Hardenberg. After this letter, Jacobson had a personal conference with the Chancellor (Freund, I, 222).

48. Jacobson to Sack, Feb. 15, 1811 (Freund, II, 430 ff.). Sack was a State Privy-Councillor and Chief of Police in the Ministry of the Interior, a very important office.

49. Freund, I, 223.

50. Silberstein, "Vorgeschichte," pp. 104-5.

51. *Sulamith,* III, No. 1, pp. 3-4.

52. Lazarus, p. 47.

53. *Sulamith,* II, No. 1, p. 10.

54. This "Consistorial School" was opened on August 15, 1809, Napoleon's birthday.

55. This projected seminary was first announced on April 26, 1809, but was not opened till September 23, 1810.

56. Cf. Auerbach, *Halberstadt,* p. 141.

57. *Meassef,* 1810, German supplement, p. 14; Lazarus, p. 18. For the educational activities of Jacobson and his friends, see the following: Horwitz, *Westfalen,* pp. 54-76; Lazarus, pp. 42-75; Jost, "Vor einem halben Jahrhundert," p. 162; Zunz, *GV,* pp. 470 ff.; *Sulamith,* I, No. 1, p. 287; Jost, *Allgemeine Geschichte,* p. 533.

58. Note in the following retrospect of Jewry by Peter Beer the intertwining of civil and religious improvement with adjustment and assimilation. Jewry is in darkness and is being brought back to light and humanity by the enlightened Jewish and non-Jewish leaders. Jacobson shared the following view of Beer: "Joseph [II of Austria] starts the work of regeneration of this people, and the majority of the rulers of Europe follow. Mendelssohn sets ablaze the lamp of Enlightenment, and there is light in Israel! Beginning of intellectual, religious, moral and civil reform of the Jews. Great Sanhedrin in Paris. Partial improvement of the religious cult and education. Inner and outer striving toward religious and civil improvement. Vigorous push toward assimilation with the other peoples" (*Sulamith,* VI, No. 2, pp. 305-6).

59. *Sulamith,* IV, No. 1, pp. 185 ff.

60. Stern, *Geschichte,* pp. 182 ff.; Jost, *Judenthum,* p. 324.

61. Horwitz, "Charakteristik," pp. 392-93.

62. Elbogen, pp. 394-95; Dubnow, II, 69-70.

63. Fraenkel, Wolf, Salomon in Dessau; Wolfssohn in Breslau; Kley in Hamburg.

64. Stern, *Geschichte,* p. 170.

65. Ruelf, XVIII, No. 46; Zimmermann, p. 99.

66. *Sulamith,* III, No. 1, p. 10; Lazarus, pp. 58 ff.; Zunz, *GV,* p. 475.

67. But cf. Stern, *Geschichte,* pp. 168-69. I disagree with Stern here that change was unconscious and without intention. The consistory decrees of 1810 show he was determined to legislate his reforms into Jewish practice in Westphalia.

68. It was built in 1805 and dedicated on July 17, 1810. The statement of Zimmermann, p. 113, that it was dedicated on July 20, 1810, is an error.

69. *Sulamith,* III, No. 1, p. 363.

70. Kleinschmidt, "Jacobson," pp. 205 ff.; Graetz, XI, 385; Stern, *Geschichte,* p. 173. A. Stern, in *AZJ,* LXXIV, 511 ff., gives an outline of the service at Seesen. It is a complete break with the past. There is much German, and there are considerable omissions, including the musaf prayer.

71. *Sulamith,* III, No. 1, pp. 298 ff.

72. A decree issued on January 18, 1810, by the consistory permitted

all Jews to use legumes, certain vegetables, and all sorts of sugar, tea, and tobacco on the Passover. The motivation of this dispensation was that the soldiers should not be compelled to eat leavened food; that they must have plenty of permissible food to eat and thus to fulfill their duties as citizens. The dispensation was grounded on talmudic and rabbinic law, and great legal authorities were quoted to establish this decision (*Sulamith*, III, No. 1, pp. 15 ff.). No attempt is made here to break with rabbinism as a source of authority. This decree was necessary now probably because of the Continental Blockade.

73. Confirmation was introduced to help children live according to the religious and moral law and loyally to conform to the statutes of the land. The ceremony was developed in Westphalia. Ehrenberg, however, had confirmed a boy at Wolfenbuettel as early as August, 1807 (Zunz, *Ehrenberg*, p. 39). In Dessau, Mendelssohn's old home, confirmation for boys alone was permissible if the parents requested it, but by a decree of April 26, 1809, the ceremony was extended in Westphalia to include girls. The first public confirmation with choir and instrumental accompaniment was held probably in Cassel, in 1810, on a Sabbath in the community synagogue. It was felt that the bar mizvah ceremony taught nothing. Confirmation would help fight the inroads of irreligion; it would strengthen love for the faith. It would help children to know Judaism (Lazarus, p. 24; Horwitz, *Westfalen*, pp. 63-64; *Sulamith*, I, No. 1, pp. 487 ff.; III, No. 1, p. 11; VIII, No. 1, pp. 279-80).

74. This decree was issued on August 17, 1810 (Horwitz, *Westfalen*, pp. 58-62).

75. This decree was issued on September 24, 1810. For the decree, cf. *Sulamith*, III, No. 1, pp. 366 ff.

76. Elbogen, p. 398.

77. Horwitz, *Westfalen*, pp. 70 ff., dates this decree July 5, 1811. In his "Neue Beitraege," p. 728, he dates it July 4th.

78. *Sulamith*, IV, No. 1, pp. 185 ff. Freund, II, 431-32: Jacobson to Sack, February 15, 1811.

79. Jost, *Gesch. der Israeliten*, p. 149; *Judenthum*, p. 326, note; Lazarus, pp. 69-70.

80. Jost, "Vor einem halben Jahrhundert," p. 160.

81. Lazarus, pp. 49, 74.

82. Cf. Philippson, *Skizzen*, p. 98.

83. Zuckermann, p. 20; Lazarus, pp. 25, 95; Jost, *Judenthum*, p. 327; Auerbach, *Halberstadt*, pp. 222-23; Horwitz, *Westfalen*, pp. 62, 68, 76 ff.

84. Cf. also *Sulamith*, VII, No. 2, pp. 214-26.

85. Steinhardt, *Dibre Iggeret:* "Hakdamah."

86. *Ibid.:* Questions Nos. 1, 3, 5, 6, 10.

87. Zuckermann, p. 17.

88. Auerbach, *Halberstadt*, pp. 140-46. It is interesting to note how these stories cluster around the Hirsch family, the arch-proponents of Orthodoxy in Northern Germany. Aron Hirsch was the father-in-law of the distinguished Israel Hildesheimer, the founder of the Neo-Orthodox school in Northern Germany.

89. Auerbach, *Halberstadt*, pp. 222-24.

90. *Ibid.*, pp. 219-22.

91. *Ibid.*, pp. 215 ff. The protest of the Fuerth rabbinate against the consistorial Passover dispensation may be found in *Jahrb. d. J. Lit. Gesell.*, VI, 227-29.

92. This is the subtitle of *Sulamith*, their official organ. It is instructive to note that the first two volumes of this periodical—Leipzig-Dessau, 1806-1809—carried the subtitle: "A periodical to further culture and humanity in the Jewish Nation." The third volume, published in Cassel, in French Westphalia, 1810, changed the phrase "in the Jewish Nation" to "among the Israelites." About twenty years later the subtitle was merely "a periodical."

93. This did not stop an enthusiastic admirer, however, from dedicating a sermon to him: "the greatest scholar and orator of Germany." Jost, "Vor einem halben Jahrhundert," p. 162. I am sure that Jacobson did not resent the dedication.

94. Zunz, *GV*, p. 475; Jost, *Judenthum*, pp. 324-31; Auerbach, *Halberstadt*, p. 150; Graetz, XI, 281, 288 ff., 386; Dubnow, II, 70; Jost, *Gesch. der Israeliten*, pp. 138 ff.; Stern, *Geschichte*, pp. 156, 162, 185; Philippson, *Neueste Geschichte*, I, 159; Horwitz, "Charakteristik," p. 392; Horwitz, *Westfalen*, p. 62; Lazarus, pp. 70-71; Jost, "Vor einem halben Jahrhundert," pp. 158-60.

95. Lazarus, p. 77.

96. Zimmermann, p. 114.

97. Horwitz, *Westfalen*, pp. 91 ff.

98. Sabel Eger, rabbi of Brunswick, in Auerbach, *Halberstadt*, p. 217, and Lazarus Riesser, in *ZGJD*, I, 370 ff., speak of this value. D. Philipson, p. 25.

99. Jost, *Allgemeine Geschichte*, pp. 511-12.

100. Stern, *Geschichte*, pp. 193-94.

101. Cf. also Philippson, *Neueste Geschichte*, I, 164; Zunz, *GV*, 474-75.

102. Jost, *Allgemeine Geschichte,* p. 535.

103. He maintained residence in several places. He continued to live at first in Brunswick. He also had rooms at Seesen, and a home in Cassel. The family estate was, however, at this time at Woeltingerode, near historic Goslar.

104. The Oker Department sent him as the Representative of Trade and Industry.

105. Kleinschmidt, *Geschichte,* p. 145, says that he pretended to be a prelate of the Church when he attempted to comfort an old nun in one of the cloisters which he had bought. This statement is very improbable. There was no need for such an action, and Jacobson would never have resorted to an unnecessary and unworthy subterfuge. Kleinschmidt should have known this was not true, for he states, p. 144, that Jacobson gave 100 francs for life to the nuns because he felt that the settlement made by the state with them was insufficient! Jacobson has been subject to anti-Jewish attack from his own day to the present moment. During the French occupation of Westphalia, the German people had neither the desire nor the opportunity to bother themselves with the Jews. After the fall of the Kingdom of Westphalia in 1813, as the anti-French reaction set in, the Jews, who had been favored by the French, again became the subject of attack. Jacobson was not spared in the anonymous mock-heroic diatribes of the day (cf. Zimmermann, pp. 114-15; Lazarus, p. 76). He has also been attacked by modern German anti-Semitic writers (cf. Kernholt, pp. 72 ff.).

106. Lazarus, p. 19.

107. Kohut, p. 29. It was during the Westphalian period that Jacob Weil wrote and dedicated his *Fragmente aus dem Talmud* (Frankfort on the Main, 1809) to Jacobson. The dedication, spread over five pages, is interesting, because typical. It glorifies "Jacobssohn," who has devoted his intellect, heart, and wealth to the furtherance of culture, humanity, and mankind. The motto of the book is a sentence from Voltaire that virtue lies not in belief, but in justice and doing good. Jacobson subscribed for twenty-five copies of this apologetic work.

108. Lazarus, pp. 15-16. Both honors in November, 1812.

109. April 10, 1808. Zimmermann, p. 113.

110. Ruelf, XIX, No. 1.

111. Cohen, pp. 130-31.

112. *Sulamith,* III, No. 2, pp. 10 ff. For his private life, cf. also Zimmermann, pp. 112-15; Kleinschmidt, "Jacobson," pp. 208-10; Lazarus, pp. 15 ff.

BERLIN

1. Zimmermann, p. 115.

2. The suggestions of Abraham Muhr, of Plesse, are obviously influenced by the ideas of Jacobson as expressed in the Westphalian consistory (Geiger, *Geschichte*, II, 217-19).

3. Jost, *Neuere Geschichte*, III, 11-14; Friedrich, p. 5; Bernfeld, *Toledot*, p. 66; Geiger, II, pp. 211-13; Jost, "Vor einem halben Jahrhundert," p. 165; *Allgemeine Geschichte*, pp. 536-37; *Judenthum*, p. 331; Stern, *Geschichte*, pp. 175, 187-88; Elbogen, p. 400.

4. Lesser, p. 73; chronological table after p. 97.

5. Graetz, XI, 318; Jost, *Neuere Geschichte*, I, 47; *Allgemeine Deutsche Biographie*, XIII, 619.

6. *Sulamith*, IV, No. 2, pp. 66-70.

7. Friedlaender did not in reality approve of the Jacobson service. He believed that it was brilliant, but lacked true warmth and inner depth (Ritter, p. 142; D. Philipson, pp. 33 ff.).

8. *Sulamith*, IV, No. 2, pp. 66-70; Zunz, *GV*, p. 475; Jost, *Judenthum*, pp. 331-32; Stern, *Geschichte*, p. 175; Jost, *Neuere Geschichte*, III, 11-14; Graetz, XI, 387; Bernfeld, *Toledot*, pp. 71-72.

9. Geiger, *Geschichte*, I, 165 ff.; II, 219 ff.

10. Zunz, *GV*, p. 476.

11. Jost, *Annalen*, 1839, p. 226.

12. Ruth 2:4; Bernfeld, *Toledot*, p. 271.

13. Bernfeld, *Toledot*, pp. 73-75; Appendix I, pp. 268 ff.; Geiger, *Geschichte*, II, 221-23; Elbogen, p. 401.

14. Geiger, *Geschichte*, I, 166-68; Roenne and Simon, p. 93.

15. Auerbach, *Judenthum*, p. 471.

16. Cf. Geiger, *Geschichte*, I, 152.

17. Stern, *Geschichte*, pp. 193-94.

18. Graetz, XI, 387; Philippson, *Neueste Geschichte*, I, 166; Jost, *Neuere Geschichte*, III, 11-14. For sermons of the time, see Salomon, *Auswahl*, and Zunz, *Predigten*, No. XIV.

19. Jost, *Annalen*, 1839, p. 243.

20. Dubnow, I, 217.

21. Jost, *Judenthum*, p. 333.

22. Strodtmann, I, 315 ff.; Maybaum, pp. 9-19; Heine, I, earlier letters.

23. Although Jacobson apparently had no real understanding of the goal of Zunz, yet he encouraged Zunz to visit him. The Hebrew Union College Museum possesses a written invitation of Jacobson inviting "Dr. Zuntz" to breakfast.

24. *Sulamith*, V, No. 2, p. 197; Jost, *Neuere Geschichte*, III, 21.

25. *ZGJD*, I, 368 ff.

26. Elbogen, pp. 402-10; Stern, *Geschichte*, p. 177; Bernfeld, *Toledot*, pp. 72-87, 275-80; Jost, *Judenthum*, p. 336; Graetz, XI, 389 ff.; Dubnow, II, 73; D. Philipson, pp. 41 ff.

27. Graetz, XI, 392 ff.

28. Stern, *Geschichte*, p. 177.

29. Strodtmann, I, 294-95, 316.

30. Graetz, XI, 409-12.

31. Bernfeld, *Toledot*, p. 87. Caro also benefited from the largess of Jacobson, *Ha-Asif*, V (Warsaw, 1889), 69.

32. Jost, *Allgemeine Geschichte*, pp. 542-44; Lippmann, p. 22.

33. *Sulamith*, VII, No. 1, pp. 278-79; Stern, *Geschichte*, p. 179.

34. *Sulamith*, VII, No. 2, pp. 39 ff.

35. Jeannette Cohen was born in Hanover in 1801 and died in Berlin in 1871. This marriage was blessed with four children, two sons and two daughters. The daughters died young. All in all, he had ten children, six boys and four girls. Cf. Berliner, Table 6.

36. Donath, pp. 179 ff. The holdings and activities of Jacobson in Mecklenburg are treated in some detail in the work of Schnee, II, 109-63; IV, 56-57. In his chapter on Jacobson the author has in effect written a biography. Schnee entitles this section: "Der Geheime Finanzrat Israel Jacobson, der Vorkaempfer der Judenemanzipation." Actually, Jacobson's role as an emancipator is not described here in great detail, and very little is said of him as a religious reformer. The author points out that it is not his purpose to deal with the religious work and accomplishments of this notable court Jew.

Schnee documents the fact that Jacobson was an exceptionally large landowner with extensive holdings in the Mecklenburg, Brunswick, and Westphalian regions. It is quite obvious that this Jewish businessman had ambitions to become a landed gentleman and to enjoy the political privileges associated with such properties. The Mecklenburg estates resented the intrusion of this man, whom they deemed an interloper, and they went out of their way to exclude him as a legislator.

Heinrich Schnee's work is particularly helpful in the economic area, for he has concentrated his researches primarily on Jacobson as a court banker. The author has scoured the archives of Germany in Berlin-Dahlem, Schwerin, Wolfenbuettel, Hannover, Karlsruhe, Wiesbaden, Brunswick, and Darmstadt, and has also examined documents in The Hague. Much of this material is new, and we are very grateful to him for the data which he has uncovered. He has helped us to redress the balance in evaluating Jacobson. We think of him only as a religious reformer and forget that he was primarily a very distinguished banker with national and international connections.

The author shows us that it was Jacobson's in-laws, the Samsons of Wolfenbuettel, who started him on his career and taught him the business of supplying the financial needs of the German courts. Obviously, they trained him well. With their aid and influence, and with assistance, too, from his father, who was by no means a poor man, Jacobson made rapid progress. He was very ambitious and possessed the drive and energy to match his hopes and his exceptional capacities. He was already a successful financier when he was not much more than thirty years of age. In the relatively short period of less than two decades as a banker, investor, land entrepreneur, and capitalist he accumulated an estate of about 1,000,000 talers. For the Germany of that day this was great wealth.

At an early stage of his career he became involved in large state loans. When the invading French occupied Brunswick they imposed a levy of over 5,000,000 francs on the land. Jacobson handled this financial operation for the state. When Jerome came to power in the Kingdom of Westphalia, Jacobson became one of his chief financial agents and negotiated loans for him running into very substantial sums. Because of these business transactions the Jewish financier was undoubtedly in a position to exert great political power. Unlike most of his Jewish banker contemporaries, he used that power consistently to further the emancipation of his fellow-Jews. He was exceedingly proud of his ancestral heritage and was determined to do what he could for his disabled coreligionists. He was devoted to them. He strove vigorously to ameliorate their civic and political, cultural and economic status in Brunswick, Westphalia, and Mecklenburg, and in the Prussia of Hardenberg. As a banker and philanthropist who was most eager to advance the status of the Jews about him, he might well have served as a prototype for the German-born American financier, Jacob H. Schiff.

The picture of Jacobson the businessman that is delineated here is anything but a sympathetic one. The author states that this man exploited the juncture of political circumstances to achieve wealth and power ruthlessly. This is a harsh value judgment which, in my opinion, is not borne out by the evidence presented. Jacobson was a tough-minded banker; it was his business to make the best deals he could, especially when negotiating with officials who resented him—if they did not despise him—because he was a Jew. In making loans he never forgot that he was a banker, not the president of a free-loan society. Schnee himself pointed out that Jacobson was more moderate in his charges than some of his Christian competitors (IV, 56-57). That is why he was able to compete successfully.

37. Ruelf, XIX, No. 2. The documents in question were translated into English by Enelow. *The Jewish Exponent,* February 23, 1934, *sub* Correspondence.

38. Philippson, *Skizzen,* II, 167-68, 216-17. It was about this time that Jacobson was intimate with Peter Friedrich von Uechtritz. This dramatist, who associated with Heine and other distinguished Jews, dedicated *Die Babyloner in Jerusalem* to Jacobson. Zirndorf, p. 105.

39. Lazarus, p. 20; Zimmerman, p. 115; Zunz, *GV,* p. 479; Jost, *Neuere Geschichte,* III, 53; *Sulamith,* VII, No. 2, pp. 39 ff.; Ritter, p. 174. The necrology of the Berlin Jewish Community is found in *Sulamith,* VII, No. 1, pp. 427 ff.

The following opinion was submitted to me by Dr. H. B. Weiss, of Cincinnati, on the basis of materials which I put at his disposal. The opinion is, of course, conjectural:

Briefly from the physical description of the man one could infer that probably, fairly early in life, say at the age of forty or fifty, Jacobson had developed hypertension (known as high blood pressure), which after persisting for some time, had in all probability produced Bright's disease, chronic nephritis. With his history of gout and rheumatism one could also infer that he was an overeater. [This is hardly borne out by our knowledge of the simplicity of the home life of Jacobson.] This, of course, goes hand in hand with his obesity and the diseases of degeneration, as hypertension and nephritis go with obesity. This type of man was very apt to be diabetic although there are not enough significant signs obtainable to warrant this inference. The nervous shock he received at fifty could easily be associated with a weakened heart and hypertension. The fact that shortly afterwards he developed mental deterioration might substantiate the diagnosis of arteriosclerosis. Sixty is not a ripe old age but it is about the time that large men die from degenerative diseases. The type of baths that he had been taking, such as saline, iron, earthy and sulphur, are probably not of any significance since individuals at that time, and at this time, have taken baths for many things, the type of water usually incidental. Psychologically it is much more difficult to make any sort of analysis here. Personally I feel that a tall, heavy man of his description would be very vain, perhaps he might be determined, probably would like to be "boss" of everything that he was interested in, although he would also quite likely be kindly, courteous, and generous. This type of person would be sensitive and would be greatly aggrieved at remarks that he considered insulting. As far as his mental deterioration later in life is concerned, this is something that comes to many men when their circulation and vital organs do not seem to function properly.

40. Cf. Silberstein, "Testament," p. 109, Note 7.

41. *Ibid.,* p. 105.

42. Graetz, XI, 403.

43. Zunz, *GV,* pp. 478 ff.; Graetz, XI, 398; Elbogen, p. 406; Jost, *Allgemeine Geschichte,* pp. 537-38, 545; Seligmann, p. 87.

44. Elbogen, pp. 410-11.

45. *Hamburg Prayer Book* (1819), "Preface"; Seligmann, p. 83. In 1835, Gotthold Salomon, one of the preachers of the Hamburg Temple, published a volume of sermons, *Moses, der Mann Gottes.* He dedicated this book to Jacobson and thanked him in bombastic verse for introducing music and the vernacular into the services.

In 1818, the Florida pioneer Moses E. Levy hoped to initiate a religious and educational reformation among the 3,000 Jews of the United States. In order to secure financial assistance, Levy was prepared to travel to Europe and seek help there from notable Jews. He hoped that Jacobson would rally to his support, for he "is rich and nearly inclined to our way of thinking" (M. E. Levy, N. Y., to Samuel Myers, Norfolk, Va., Nov. 1, 1818, copy in the American Jewish Archives). In 1847, a Jacobsohn Society, probably named after Jacobson, was established by a group of young Jews in Buffalo. It had its own cemetery and may have been a sick-care and burial confraternity (Selig Adler and Thomas E. Connolly, *From Ararat to Suburbia: The History of the Jewish Community of Buffalo* [Phila., 1960], see Index under "Jacobsohn Society").

46. Cf. Zunz, *GV,* p. 482.

47. Elbogen, pp. 439 ff.

Index

Z